Econversations
Today's Students Discuss Today's Issues

John J. Walters

Christopher D. Appel

Crystal A. Callahan

Nicholas L. Centanni

Steven A. Maex

Daniel G. O'Neill

Edited by
Stephen J. K. Walters, Ph.D.
Loyola University Maryland

D1329739

PEARSON

Boston   Columbus   Indianapolis   New York   San Francisco   Upper Saddle River
Amsterdam   Cape Town   Dubai   London   Madrid   Milan   Munich   Paris   Montreal   Toronto
Delhi   Mexico City   São Paulo   Sydney   Hong Kong   Seoul   Singapore   Taipei   Tokyo

The Pearson Series in Economics

Abel/Bernanke/Croushore
*Macroeconomics**

Bade/Parkin
*Foundations of Economics**

Berck/Helfand
The Economics of the Environment

Bierman/Fernandez
Game Theory with Economic Applications

Blanchard
*Macroeconomics**

Blau/Ferber/Winkler
The Economics of Women, Men, and Work

Boardman/Greenberg/Vining/Weimer
Cost-Benefit Analysis

Boyer
Principles of Transportation Economics

Branson
Macroeconomic Theory and Policy

Brock/Adams
The Structure of American Industry

Bruce
Public Finance and the American Economy

Carlton/Perloff
Modern Industrial Organization

Case/Fair/Oster
*Principles of Economics**

Caves/Frankel/Jones
World Trade and Payments: An Introduction

Chapman
Environmental Economics: Theory, Application, and Policy

Cooter/Ulen
Law & Economics

Downs
An Economic Theory of Democracy

Ehrenberg/Smith
Modern Labor Economics

Farnham
Economics for Managers

Folland/Goodman/Stano
The Economics of Health and Health Care

Fort
Sports Economics

Froyen
Macroeconomics

Fusfeld
The Age of the Economist

Gerber
*International Economics**

González-Rivera
Forecasting for Economics and Business

Gordon
*Macroeconomics**

Greene
Econometric Analysis

Gregory
Essentials of Economics

Gregory/Stuart
Russian and Soviet Economic Performance and Structure

Hartwick/Olewiler
The Economics of Natural Resource Use

Heilbroner/Milberg
The Making of the Economic Society

Heyne/Boettke/Prychitko
The Economic Way of Thinking

Hoffman/Averett
Women and the Economy: Family, Work, and Pay

Holt
Markets, Games, and Strategic Behavior

Hubbard/O'Brien
*Economics**
*Money, Banking, and the Financial System**

Hubbard/O'Brien/Rafferty
*Macroeconomics**

Hughes/Cain
American Economic History

Husted/Melvin
International Economics

Jehle/Reny
Advanced Microeconomic Theory

Johnson-Lans
A Health Economics Primer

Keat/Young
Managerial Economics

Klein
Mathematical Methods for Economics

Krugman/Obstfeld/Melitz
*International Economics: Theory & Policy**

Laidler
The Demand for Money

Leeds/von Allmen
The Economics of Sports

Leeds/von Allmen/Schiming
*Economics**

Lipsey/Ragan/Storer
*Economics**

Lynn
Economic Development: Theory and Practice for a Divided World

Miller
*Economics Today**
Understanding Modern Economics

Miller/Benjamin
The Economics of Macro Issues

Miller/Benjamin/North
The Economics of Public Issues

Mills/Hamilton
Urban Economics

Mishkin
*The Economics of Money, Banking, and Financial Markets**
*The Economics of Money, Banking, and Financial Markets, Business School Edition**
*Macroeconomics: Policy and Practice**

Murray
Econometrics: A Modern Introduction

Nafziger
The Economics of Developing Countries

O'Sullivan/Sheffrin/Perez
*Economics: Principles, Applications, and Tools**

Parkin
*Economics**

Perloff
*Microeconomics**
*Microeconomics: Theory and Applications with Calculus**

Perman/Common/McGilvray/Ma
Natural Resources and Environmental Economics

Phelps
Health Economics

Pindyck/Rubinfeld
*Microeconomics**

Riddell/Shackelford/Stamos/Schneider
Economics: A Tool for Critically Understanding Society

Ritter/Silber/Udell
*Principles of Money, Banking & Financial Markets**

Roberts
The Choice: A Fable of Free Trade and Protection

Rohlf
Introduction to Economic Reasoning

Ruffin/Gregory
Principles of Economics

Sargent
Rational Expectations and Inflation

Sawyer/Sprinkle
International Economics

Scherer
Industry Structure, Strategy, and Public Policy

Schiller
The Economics of Poverty and Discrimination

Sherman
Market Regulation

Silberberg
Principles of Microeconomics

Stock/Watson
Introduction to Econometrics

Studenmund
Using Econometrics: A Practical Guide

Tietenberg/Lewis
Environmental and Natural Resource Economics
Environmental Economics and Policy

Todaro/Smith
Economic Development

Waldman
Microeconomics

Waldman/Jensen
Industrial Organization: Theory and Practice

Walters/Walters/Appel/Callahan/Centanni/Maex/O'Neill
Econversations: Today's Students Discuss Today's Issues

Weil
Economic Growth

Williamson
Macroeconomics

Editor in Chief: Donna Battista
Senior Acquisitions Editor: Noel Seibert
Senior Editorial Project Manager: Carolyn Terbush
Editorial Assistant: Emily Brodeur
Development Editor: Deepa Chungi
Director of Marketing: Maggie Moylan
Executive Marketing Manager: Lori DeShazo
Marketing Assistant: Kim Lovato
Senior Managing Editor: Nancy Fenton
Production Project Manager: Alison Eusden
Production Manager: Maggie Brobeck
Art Director: Jon Boylan

Text and Cover Designer: Jon Boylan
Manager, Rights and Permissions: Michael Joyce
**Manager, Cover Visual Research and
  Permissions:** Rachel Youdelman
Media Director: Susan Schoenberg
Lead Media Project Manager: Melissa Honig
**Full-Service Project Management and
  Composition:** Aptara®, Inc./Jogender Taneja

Text Font: Palatino LT Std

Cover Photos Credits (left to right): V. J. Matthew/ Shutterstock; Lenetstan/Shutterstock; R. Gino Santa Maria/Shutterstock; Audfriday13/Fotolia.

Credits and acknowledgments borrowed from other sources and reproduced, with permission, in this textbook appear on the appropriate page within text.

Many of the designations by manufacturers and sellers to distinguish their products are claimed as trademarks. Where those designations appear in this book, and the publisher was aware of a trademark claim, the designations have been printed in initial caps or all caps.

Library of Congress Cataloging-in-Publication Data
Econversations: today's students discuss today's issues / John J. Walters . . . [et al.]; edited by Stephen J.K. Walters.—1st ed.
   p. cm.
 ISBN-13: 978-0-13-254466-5
 ISBN-10: 0-13-254466-0
 1. Economics. I. Walters, John J. II. Walters, Stephen John Kasabuski, 1953-
   HB171.5.E359 2013
   330—dc23   2012019805

Student Edition
ISBN-10: 0-13-254466-0
ISBN-13: 978-0-13-254466-5

Instructor's Review Copy
ISBN-10: 0-13-254468-7
ISBN-13: 978-0-13-254468-9

CONTENTS

CHAPTER 1

Live Together, Die Alone
Competition, Cooperation, and International Trade   **1**

Chapter Highlights
Gains from Trade • Competition • Protectionism • The Law of Comparative Advantage

CHAPTER 2

The War on the Economy
Stimulus Spending and Job "Creation"   **12**

Chapter Highlights
Opportunity Cost • Economic Stimulus • Business Cycles • Gross Domestic Product • The Keynesian Multiplier

CHAPTER 6
All You Can Eat
Demand and Supply at the Healthcare Buffet   **54**

Chapter Highlights
*Marginal Benefits and Costs • Health Economics • Moral Hazard
• Adverse Selection • The Samaritan's Dilemma*

CHAPTER 7
Green Is the New Black
Environmental Problems and Policy   **66**

Chapter Highlights
*The Tragedy of the Commons • The Coase Theorem • Negative and Positive
Externalities • Environmental Regulation • Cost-Benefit Analysis*

CHAPTER 8

Santa, Inc.

Chapter Highlights
Profit (Economic vs. Accounting) • *Predatory Pricing* • *Monopoly*
• *Scale Economies and Diseconomies* • *Price Fixing*

CHAPTER 9

Spiking the Punch

Chapter Highlights
Financial Markets • *Interest Rates and Risk* • *Principal-Agent
Problems* • *Incentives* • *Moral Hazard*

CHAPTER 10

Stairway to . . . Sweatshops?
What Foreign Factories Mean for You, Me, and the Developing World

Chapter Highlights
*Market Competition • Outsourcing • Economic Development
• Costs and Production • Fair Trade*

CHAPTER 11

Why Men Love Tools
Poverty at the Personal and National Levels

Chapter Highlights
*Poverty Threshold / Poverty Rate • Investment • Physical Capital
• Human Capital • Economic Freedom and Growth*

CHAPTER 12

Land of the Free
Regulation, Redistribution, and Rights   **128**

Chapter Highlights
*Tradeoffs • Optimization vs. Maximization • Equity vs. Efficiency
• Income Redistribution • Insurance*

Student Foreword

A Book for Students, by Students

The French have a great name for one of my all-time favorite activities from college. You grab a bottle of wine (or two) and a few of your best friends. Then you sit around a table and *refaire le monde*—you remake the world. You discuss all the problems that you see around you and how you would fix them. That's one of the great things about college—you get to engage in great conversations with all kinds of smart, motivated people.

Early one morning before our midlevel economics class, my friend Crystal and I were doing just that, fueling our discussion with heavy doses of caffeine instead of alcohol and antioxidants. I floated the idea of compiling all the issues that we found ourselves discussing regularly into a student-authored book.

Fast-forward one semester, and we had become a team of six (plus one professor). Each of us was on a mission to pick two of the issues we were most passionate about, to figure out where most discussions devolved into unproductive arguments, and to write short chapters that could serve as the start of much more reasoned and amicable debates than the ones we often experienced.

How do you explain to someone who knows deep down in her gut that drugs are bad that you are on her side when you say that America needs to reevaluate fighting a war against them? How do you assure a sweatshops protester that you also share his passion for better working conditions in Third World countries—while continuing to shop at Wal-Mart? And how can you claim to be in favor of better healthcare in America while simultaneously advocating fewer regulations and more privatization?

The answer, as we found out time and time again, is that you don't—at least, not easily. It's not that these positions cannot be held. It's just that holding these beliefs can make you something of a pariah in the idealistic world of college activism, and you need to choose your words very carefully in such debates to avoid being immediately labeled as either an absolute idiot or extremely selfish.

The goal is to start conversations that will unearth new solutions to old problems. And that's just it. None of these problems are new. While they are certainly current issues faced by our country and our economy today, nearly all of them have been around for decades—even centuries. Over time, the details have changed, but the fundamental scenarios have remained the same, and so has the rhetoric. It's time to create an environment in which students, the future leaders of our nation, can discuss and debate these issues so that change can finally come.

We do not differ in our desires. In almost all cases, we want the same things: a cleaner, safer, more prosperous, and happier world. We diverge, however, in the paths that we wish to take to create this better place. Our training in economics reshapes the lens through which we view the world and gives us a perspective that few naturally tap into, save on those occasions when economics and "common sense" coincide. But the important thing to take from this book is not that there is a right and wrong to each issue but that there are new, creative ways of solving a problem that may not always be readily apparent.

In this book, you'll find short chapters about how environmentalism has made green the new black, how the war on drugs can make sticks cost $1,200, and how the healthcare debate is like a Chinese buffet. Each chapter covers a topic (or two) that would also be covered by your average economics principles textbook, but with a different and, we hope, more accessible perspective. Are we always going to be right in our reasoning? Of course not. We were students when we wrote this, just like you are now. We like to think that we have everything figured out, that whatever side we've chosen is the "right" one. But that's not always the case.

What the professors aren't telling you is that they're students, too. We all are. Everyone is still learning, until the day they choose to stop. Whether we all agree about the solutions to these problems isn't important. The important thing is to keep having conversations about them—that we don't just throw our hands up in the air and say, "That's just the way it's always been."

And, as students, it's important that we stay informed and participate as well.

—John J. Walters
Baltimore, Maryland, USA
July 2012

Instructor Foreword

Pick up the Hammer

In every goofy Adam Sandler movie there seems to be a scene where our hero faces an epic challenge and insurmountable odds. A crowd nevertheless urges him on, at which point Sandler's old *Saturday Night Live* buddy Rob Schneider usually makes a cameo and shouts, "You can do it!"

This is something most of us need: our own Schneider to remind us that we *can* accomplish important but difficult things. Experience (both inside and outside the classroom) has taught me that people are insecure beings. We hate to try things that we don't think we will do well. Nobody likes to be embarrassed. It's why I dance only at weddings—and then only if forced to do so by my rhythmically gifted wife. On the other hand, if we are good at something, we want to do it often—and as a result, we get even better at it. I love to teach, so I not only decided to make a career out of it, but I have apparently improved with age.[1]

A big part of that improvement came when I stopped merely *suggesting* that students should apply the tools we were discussing and instead actually took steps to ensure that they *did* so. You get better at carpentry by grabbing a hammer and pounding nails, not just listening to others talk about it. But my performance in this regard has always been spotty, in part because of that pesky insecurity problem. When I reserve more class time for student discussion, I find that many are reluctant to put their egos on the line to risk answering a question or voicing an opinion—just like I fear a dance floor.

Which brings us to this book. It is not only *for* students, but it is *by* students. Thus, every page should assure readers that "you can do it!" If you are just starting to learn about economics, it will be empowering to see how, after investing some time practicing with the tools of economic analysis as the authors have done, you will be able to take on the controversial policy issues of the day and move debates about them forward. In short, a "demonstration effect" will break down some of the inhibitions we all feel when we are trying something new.

---

1 I don't think I am delusional about this. My student evaluation scores have trended upward over time, and I got a college-wide "distinguished teaching" award only after plugging away in the classroom for 24 years.

That is not, however, the main reason these students took on this project. They wanted to write about these high-profile issues because once they had acquired key economic tools they found them indispensable in debates with their friends and classmates in dorms, coffeehouses, and, yes, bars. And they were eager to argue with a broader audience. As a teacher, I saw a happy side effect: that their willingness to argue could provoke their peers to do the same thing and thus to apply the concepts we try to put over in class. It can be intimidating to argue with a professor; with a fellow student, not so much.

Another virtue of the book is that it brings a fresh, student point of view to topics that are not only important but interesting. We know this not just because the topics appear regularly in headlines or fill time on talk shows: The student authors chose them by wandering around their campus and tuning in to the economic, political, or philosophical discussions their peers were actually having—often at high volume.

Having done that legwork, though, why not turn the actual writing over to trusted authorities like professors? Apart from addressing that insecurity issue, student authorship might help in another way: The authors' struggles with the "economic way of thinking" are fresh in their minds. They have learned how to use economic models but can still remember how they first circled them warily, perhaps misunderstood them, and then, often grudgingly, grasped them. They *question* many things that those more deeply immersed in the field might *assume* to be true (sometimes without saying so). All of which might give them an advantage in demonstrating the tools' broad usefulness. And their stories and arguments are surely more fun to read and more relevant to other students' lives than those I might relate.

Each chapter of *Econversations* builds on tools of analysis that are usually developed in a good first course in economics.[2] Some add depth to discussions that command space in textbooks (e.g., the first chapter on globalization and trade). Others take readers beyond the confines of most texts, inviting readers to apply economic logic to questions that might seem, at first glance, to be "noneconomic" (e.g., the last chapter on policies that compromise our freedom). Readers will get a heads-up about the key economic concepts used in the list of Chapter Highlights at the front of each chapter. Instructors will find brief suggestions about how to use this book as a companion to their lectures and texts in the postscript to this Foreword.

All the chapters take stands. The student authors are not fence-straddlers. They are always respectful of alternative views, however.

---

2 Readers should find, however, that they can enjoy the essays even if they are not enrolled in such a course. The authors have taken pains to make their arguments relatively jargon-free—or, at least, to make any unavoidable jargon accessible.

They have learned in many "econversations" that sneering or otherwise showing disrespect for one's interlocutor neither wins friends nor influences people.

Readers may find themselves disagreeing with the authors on many occasions. That is not a bad thing. Marshaling logic or facts to refute someone else's arguments is the very kind of engagement with the subject matter that will make one a better thinker and problem solver. And that, ultimately, is the authors' goal.

—**Stephen J.K. Walters, Ph.D**.
Loyola University Maryland
Baltimore, Maryland, USA
July 2012

A NOTE TO INSTRUCTORS: SUGGESTIONS FOR USE

Econversations is best used as supplementary reading for an initial course in economics principles. Whether that's micro, macro, or a one-semester survey course, this book focuses on the topics that interest students most and invites them to apply the analytic tools they are acquiring to relevant and important current issues.

Which chapters to assign and when to assign them will, of course, be a matter of personal preference. Some suggestions along these lines are posted in an online Instructor's Manual at Pearson's Instructor's Resource Center at www.pearsonhighered.com/irc.

While the order of the chapters often follows that of a standard survey textbook, each was written to be freestanding—readable without depending on terminology or tools discussed earlier. Consider, for example, Chapter 7 ("Green Is the New Black"), which addresses environmental issues. It could be assigned quite early, since some texts introduce concepts like the Tragedy of the Commons in their first or second chapters as a way of highlighting the role that property rights can play in resource allocation. Or it could be assigned later, after the market process has been discussed, to illustrate potential market failure—or even further on, to apply cost concepts and cost-benefit analysis.

For guidance on timing, the Table of Contents lists the five most important economic concepts readers will encounter in each chapter. Those Highlights are repeated at the beginning of each chapter so students can link the reading to their text and class discussions. Instructors can also scan those lists and quickly assess how and where each chapter fits into his or her particular course.

Half of the dozen chapters (1, 2, 3, 9, 10, and 11) have content that might be found in a course devoted to macroeconomics, and two of these (2 and 9) focus on macro-oriented material. In the rest, the goal has been to stress the economic concepts that constitute the foundations of economic analysis—opportunity cost, gains from trade, market dynamics and potential failures, the role of institutions, etc.—so that students in their first econ class will be able to see the broad utility of the tools they are acquiring.

All the chapters include a section titled Read On/Join Up. The student authors don't expect all readers to agree with their take on these crucial issues, and here they recommend readings that provide contrary points of view as well as material that provides more in-depth, detailed analysis than the chapters allow. In addition, they offer suggestions about organizations or institutions that interested and curious readers might want to investigate further. Links to the Web sites referenced can be found at the companion Web site to *Econversations*, at www.pearsonhighered.com/walters, which also includes contact information for each of the authors.

Each chapter ends with a handful of questions that will help readers to review the key concepts employed, think critically about the authors' arguments, and apply the tools acquired to additional issues. The online Instructor's Manual (again, at www.pearsonhighered.com/irc) supplies sample answers. The goal of these exercises—and, indeed, of the book itself—is to supply opportunities for students to have well-focused discussions inside or outside class and/or to craft short essays that could enhance their ability to analyze policy questions and make insightful, convincing arguments.

—**Stephen J.K. Walters, Ph.D.**
Loyola University Maryland
Baltimore, Maryland, USA
July 2012

ACKNOWLEDGMENTS

The authors and editor are enormously grateful to the following reviewers, who provided insightful suggestions and constructive criticism all along the way:

Olugbenga Ajilore, *University of Toledo*
John Blair, *Wright State University*
Jeanne Boeh, *Augsburg College*
Joseph Calhoun, *Florida State University*
Mark Funk, *University of Arkansas at Little Rock*
Lisa Giddings, *University of Wisconsin La Crosse*
Abbas P. Grammy, *California State University, Bakersfield*
Mary Kassis, *University of West Georgia*
Anthony Laramie, *Merrimack College*
Brian Lynch, *Lake Land College*
Mehrdad Madresehee, *Lycoming College*
Laura Maghoney, *Solano Community College*
John Marcis, *Coastal Carolina University*
John McArthur, *Wofford College*
Larry McCarthy, *Slippery Rock University*
Amyaz Moledina, *College of Wooster*
Diana Osborne, *Spokane Community College*
Walter Park, *American University*
Steven Pressman, *Monmouth University*
Rick D. Pretzsch, *Lone Star College Cyfair*
Randall K. Russell, *Yavapai College*
Dr. Michael T. Tasto, *Southern New Hampshire University*
Dosse Toulaboe, *Fort Hays State University*
Russel Neil Walter, *Dixie State College*

In addition, we thank Noel Seibert, Carolyn Terbush, and Deepa Chungi at Pearson Higher Education for their leadership, support, and understanding as they skillfully herded this group of cats along the trail to publication.

About the Authors

John J. Walters   Since graduating from Loyola University Maryland with a major in economics, John has been working for a local public policy institute and a venture capital firm. He hopes to continue to write economics-related nonfiction and maybe even the occasional work of fiction throughout his life—because he suspects he is not cut out for cubicle work.

Christopher D. Appel   Chris spent most of his childhood on soccer fields in New York and Connecticut before moving to Maryland to study business, economics, and Chinese at Loyola University. He began his career working for IBM in Washington, DC, and is currently employed by a smaller consulting firm based out of New York.

Crystal A. Callahan   Crystal grew up in Cherry Hill, NJ. She graduated from Loyola University Maryland in 2009 with a major in economics and a minor in philosophy. Hoping to extend her tenure as a career student, she immediately enrolled in law school after Loyola. She will earn her JD from Boston University School of Law in May 2012.

Nicholas L. Centanni   Nick was born and raised in New Jersey, or the Great Garden State, as he likes to refer to it. While a student at Loyola, he was a visible presence as a student leader and host of both television and radio programs on Loyola's campus. He is an avid "political junkie" and currently works for one of the top four accounting and consulting firms.

Steven A. Maex   Steve was born and raised in Baltimore, Maryland. A true "Baltimoron," he's an avid sports fan, particularly of his beloved Ravens and Orioles. After graduating from Loyola University in Maryland, he obtained his Certified Public Accountant certification and currently works for an accounting and consulting firm in downtown Baltimore. In his free time, he enjoys golfing as well as studying free-market economics.

Daniel G. O'Neill   Dan took his first economics class in the fall semester of his freshman year at Loyola and chose the subject as his major soon after. He graduated in 2009 with a BA in economics and Spanish, a much improved ping-pong shot, and an ongoing curiosity about the way economics relates to the real world. When he's not reading or writing about economics, you can find him in Baltimore working as an analyst for a small consulting firm.

ABOUT THE EDITOR

Stephen J. K. Walters Stephen J. K. Walters is a professor of economics at Loyola University Maryland, where he was voted Distinguished Teacher of the Year in 2005. He also serves as an economic adviser to the Baltimore Orioles and as a Fellow of Johns Hopkins University's Institute for Applied Economics, Global Health, and the Study of Business Enterprise. He earned his BA in economics at the University of Pennsylvania and his PhD at the University of California, Los Angeles.

CHAPTER 1

Live Together, Die Alone

Competition, Cooperation, and International Trade

by Christopher D. Appel

"When we try to pick out anything by itself, we find it hitched to everything else in the Universe."

—JOHN MUIR, NATURALIST, PRESERVATIONIST AND
FOUNDER OF THE SIERRA CLUB (1838–1914)

Chapter Highlights

- Gains from Trade
- Competition
- Protectionism
- The Law of Comparative Advantage

My alarm is beeping. Damn. I hate that noise. I flip the infernal thing over. Made in China. I could have guessed. I'm tempted to hit the snooze button, but the day has to start sometime; noon seems as good a time as any.

I check the tag on my favorite pillow. Who knew that German engineering could help you sleep better? My blanket? From Portugal. I thank Europe for making my bed so comfortable.

Okay, time for a shower. I grab some shampoo, out of Cincinnati, Ohio. Nice—the good ole USA is on the board. Next up, clean my teeth with a Chinese toothbrush. Shocker: My Colgate toothpaste is from Mexico. Didn't see that coming. I finish my bathroom routine and put on my Hong Kong-made blue jeans and a cotton T-shirt from El Salvador.

But hold on—the cotton likely came from one of three sources. After all, the United States, India, and China are the world's leading cotton producers. As it turns out, it's hard to find any product that was made in just one country. I slip on my sandals. Thanks, China. You wake me up, clean my teeth, and put shoes on my feet every morning.

Then I turn on my computer to check my e-mail, some news, and the weather. It's a Sony, which I know is a Japanese company, but to my surprise this $1,000 miracle machine was made in China. Only 65 years ago, Japan and China fought a brutal war. Nearly twenty million people were killed. How on earth did Sony get the Chinese and Japanese to work together on my laptop? Anyway, I'm sure its hundreds of parts came from all over the world. The copper in the electrical wires, the plastic outer casing, the LCD screen, and the motherboard probably all started somewhere other than China. Out of curiosity I check the battery: made in Singapore. And the software that makes my laptop more than a fancy paperweight came from the United States.

It's amazing how integrated and cooperative our world is. If you're skeptical, I encourage you to check the "Made in Country X" label on everything you touch tomorrow. Don't forget to substitute "Assembled" for "Made" because all the pieces and parts of what you own probably came from multiple sources. You may not have the same lazy morning routine as I do, but I am willing to bet that more than one country makes your day possible.

Peaceful cooperation between hundreds of countries and billions of people sounds pretty cool to me. Not everyone feels this way, however. In 1999, Seattle was shut down by thousands of people protesting globalization. Riot police made over 500 arrests, and the city suffered about $2.5 million in property damage. Even Starbucks was not spared the rage of protestors, who broke a store's windows and stole merchandise.[1] A few years later, a similar antiglobalization demonstration turned even more violent in Genoa, Italy. Over 50,000 people filled the streets, some throwing Molotov cocktails at police. Before it was over, 100 were wounded and one protester had been killed.[2]

Opposition to international trade is not limited to a few extremists who organize occasionally violent demonstrations. According to a 2007 survey by the Pew Research Center, only 59 percent of Americans believe world trade is good for their country.[3] That leaves 41 percent who are convinced that it's bad or not sure what to think.

Before we can understand why trade between countries is such a divisive issue—much less how it can make someone angry enough to trash a coffee shop, light a fuse on a bottle of gasoline, or confront gun-toting police—we need to consider how it really affects you, me, and people around the world.

---

1 Gillham, Patrick. "Complexity & Irony in Policing and Protesting: The World Trade Organization in Seattle." *Social Justice*, 2000, vol. 27, no. 2, pp. 212–236.

2 "G8 Summit Death Shocks Leaders." *CNN*, July 20, 2001. Protests of global economic organizations have been common in years since.

3 "Globalization: Turning Their Backs on the World." Editorial. *The Economist*. February 19, 2009.

RUMBLE IN THE BRONX

My grandfather immigrated to the United States from Germany at the end of World War II. He barely spoke English, but he was very good with his hands. He was a skilled craftsman and a trained patternmaker, and eventually he started his own factory in the Bronx. Founded in 1959, the company made cast-metal products for clients like NASA, Lockheed Martin, and Boeing. At its peak, the foundry employed about 20 local citizens, including my father. This level of entrepreneurship was an impressive accomplishment.

In the 1990s, however, things started to change. Fewer clients called, and the company had to reduce its staff. Everyone wondered where all the work had gone. Eventually my father left the company, and in the year 2000 my grandfather shut down the foundry and retired.

As you might expect, there was some genuine frustration about what had happened. That foundry was ours. It was built from the ground up by an immigrant family, and it manufactured useful, tangible products. This was the American dream come true. But that did not matter to the company's clients, who took their business to lower-cost competitors in the United States and abroad.

At the time, it was easy to blame foreign competition. But pressure from overseas was just one of many factors involved in the closing. The manufacturing sector in the United States was changing, as larger, more efficient competitors could deliver similar products at lower prices. The only domestic survivors were those capable of withstanding tighter environmental standards and a general increase in the costs of labor, utilities, and raw materials.

Given enough investment in new technology, more up-to-date production methods, and a slightly larger scale of operations, I believe my grandfather's foundry could have remained competitive. In the end, however, the domestic and foreign firms that had already made such changes, and who could subsequently offer customers lower prices for similar products, won out. My grandfather's former clients saved money by taking their business elsewhere, and those savings were eventually passed on to their customers. Would it have been better—not just for my family but for society in general—for them and their clients to pay more to save my Grandpa's company? In other words, would the world be a better place if we protected companies like my grandfather's from globalization and foreign (or even domestic) competition?

One thing we know for sure is that the threat of bankruptcy and unemployment that seems to come with increased competition gives some people a strong incentive to favor such protection. Since these consequences are felt intensely by a relatively small (and therefore easily organized) group of people, this group is more likely to translate its sentiments into action. Meanwhile, the benefits of competition and trade—such as lower prices, increased supply, and better quality—are spread out among many. Even if those of us who receive these benefits are aware of them, we might think it's our duty to keep people from suffering the adverse consequences of international competition. Should we?

CHANGE

The belief that trade causes chronic, high unemployment is very common. It's also wrong. To make this clear, we have to look at a little bit of economic history. It's also important to acknowledge that almost anything that has the potential to improve our quality of life might cause a bout of temporary unemployment.[4]

Let's deal with the history first. In a nutshell, U.S. unemployment rates generally have remained low even though international trade has increased sharply. After World War II, import taxes were reduced significantly, and the United States has imported more and more from abroad ever since. If trading with other countries caused large-scale, persistent unemployment, you would expect an increase in international trade to cause a similar increase in joblessness, but that has not happened. Figure 1.1 tells the story[5]: Since 1960, trade (as a percentage of gross domestic product, or GDP; the black line) has soared, while the unemployment rate (the grey line) has not.[6]

Still, it is undeniable that some people, particularly low-skilled workers, have become unemployed (or suffered from lower wages or slower wage growth) because of increasing international trade and outsourcing. This is because they compete directly with billions of similarly low-skilled (and low-paid) workers in foreign countries.

To see why the type of unemployment caused by competition and trade is not entirely a bad thing, it might be helpful to think about how much trade resembles ordinary technological progress. Inventing a better or cheaper way to do things isn't really very different from finding better or cheaper products in distant markets. Consider lightbulbs. Did people riot in the streets when Thomas Edison invented those little wonders? If

---

4 There are three general types of unemployment: (1) frictional: worker skills remain relevant but it takes time to switch jobs; (2) structural: worker skills are out-of-date, and retraining is necessary to find a new job; and (3) cyclical: typically associated with economic events such as recessions and depressions. The unemployment caused by international trade is likely either frictional or structural.

5 Author created Figure 1.1 based on data from the following sources: World Bank Group, *World Development Indicators & Global Development Finance.* Available at http://databank. worldbank.org; United States Bureau of Labor Statistics, *Labor Force Statistics from the Current Population Survey.* Available at http://bls.gov/cps/.

6 Another example, from more ancient history: When the Great Depression started in 1929, we responded by blaming the foreigners who were trading with us and stealing our jobs, so we raised import taxes significantly with the infamous Smoot-Hawley tariffs of 1930. Trade collapsed, but unemployment soared, reaching almost 25 percent by 1933.

Figure 1.1 More Trade ≠ More Unemployment

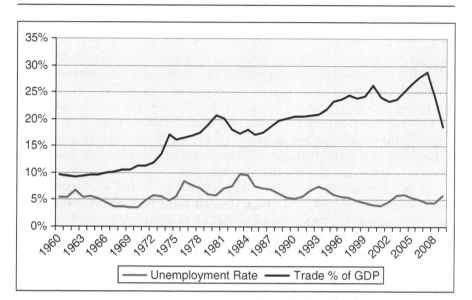

not, maybe they should have. Edison undoubtedly cost a lot of candle makers their jobs. But we still celebrate his breakthrough, because his product was cheaper, safer, and more reliable than the alternative. What's more, it probably *increased* total employment over time by making it easier to see in the dark.

Just as important, the unemployed labor and other resources required to produce candles then could be used to create something *else* that society considered more useful. If outraged candle makers had had their way and lightbulbs were made illegal or unnecessarily expensive, nighttime might be a little more romantic but a lot less productive, and the world would be poorer as a result.

Of course, technological change usually gets a free pass, while change brought about by outsourcing jobs to foreign countries is regularly attacked. Very few people want scientific progress to grind to a halt; most of us consider resisting new technology counterproductive. But opposition to international trade is just as damaging. It's just harder for people to see it that way. Why are people more understanding when an idea displaces workers than when global competition does the same thing?

Let's take a step back and think about trade that occurs between different but united states. If you walk into a car dealership and find out that the model you like was assembled in Alabama instead of Michigan, you probably wouldn't say, "Hey, Detroit has always been the Motor City; those Southerners are stealing our jobs." It's all in the American family, right? But if the same car came from South Korea, would your outlook change?[7]

If you found yourself answering "yes" to that question, you're not alone. It's extremely common for people to think a trade that crosses a national boundary is different from one that just crosses a state line. But why? It's possible that considerations of nationalism (or even race) are involved. Or, on the other hand, we might be worried about wage exploitation of foreign labor.[8] For now, though, it helps just to recognize how blurry the lines between interstate and international trade really are. Arguing that Michigan needs protection from Alabama may seem silly today. Arguing that American workers need protection from South Koreans may someday be viewed the same way.

In general, almost anything that has the potential to improve society—and, necessarily, to change it—can put pressure on people and businesses enjoying the status quo. That's just as true of competition and trade as it is of technological progress. And this can ultimately cause unemployment for the individuals whose skills are suddenly out-of-date.

This challenging and sometimes unpredictable process constantly requires people to adapt in such a way that they can better navigate a modern, globally integrated economy. Such adaptation occurs with varying levels of success and excitement in classrooms all over the world. It is also pretty easy to see in the workplace, where employees, the companies they work for, and frequently entire industries are presented with rapidly changing opportunities for which they may or may not be prepared.

My grandfather's foundry was on the front lines of such a transition. Production traditionally required my grandfather and several of his employees to look at a sketch of a prototype and then use their bare hands, molten hot metal, and dangerous machines to make a structurally sound casting. More modern methods of production, often employed by larger competitors, involved numerous foreign suppliers and a great deal of mechanical automation. Their techniques may not have been "traditional," but they enabled these competitors to fabricate new things faster and less expensively.

The challenges that my grandfather and father worked hard to overcome are similar to the larger trends faced by manufacturers throughout the developed world. Although the number of U.S. citizens employed in manufacturing fell by about 4.5 million between 1972 and 2008, industry output actually increased by close to 40 percent. Part of this increase can be attributed to technological change and access to inexpensive products

---

7 In fact, Hyundai Motor Company opened a $1.1 billion assembly plant employing over 2,000 people in Alabama in 2005. They build the popular Sonata there. So whenever we consumers decide that the Sonata is better or cheaper than the alternatives built in Detroit, maybe we're helping Alabama "steal" jobs from Michigan—in league with a South Korean company!

8 This is a topic that generates so much controversy that we've devoted an entire chapter to it. See Chapter 10, Stairway to . . . Sweatshops?

(or inputs) imported from abroad that are ultimately used in the manufacturing process.[9] As a result, throughout this period of globalization, the United States continued to rank near the top of all countries in total manufacturing output.

Pressure to change can be a good thing. At the personal level, competition and trade give us strong incentives to improve our skills and take better advantage of the resources available to us. And at the national level, trading with other countries that are at different stages of the development process or have unique resources and skill sets enables everyone to avoid doing things that we do relatively badly (meaning, at high cost) and to focus on things we do well.

ISOLATION NATION

I spent eight months in China during my junior year of college. My travels took me to poor but developing places like Xinjiang and Inner Mongolia. While these regions are breathtaking in their natural beauty, their inhabitants lead difficult lives. They have little infrastructure and insufficient water supplies, are far away from international ports, and are often plagued by corrupt local governments.

Many children in such rural areas work for their parents as soon as they are able. I met a 30-year-old woman in Guilin who had spent much of her childhood planting and harvesting rice with her family. She began to help with the daily work at age 7; by age 10 she was considered fully capable of working the same long hours as an adult. As difficult as that was, she considered her family to have been fortunate to have had a farm to work on at all.

Her childhood was defined by geographic isolation and lack of economic opportunity. Without much access to regional, national, or international markets, her parents had little choice but to put their children to work. For decades, China's government maintained a policy of closed borders and limited, carefully controlled trade. These policies prevented its billion people from applying their abundant skills to new tasks and producing goods they could exchange for the things they needed from the rest of the world, including the tools that would have made them more productive. Opponents of international trade may not think of it this way, but they're advocating the same kind of isolation that contributed to China's poverty (and made child labor in many of its rural areas a necessity) for so many years after World War II.

Even if we're capable of being "self-sufficient" as individuals, isolation from other people prevents us from reaching our full potential. It forces us to spend our limited time and resources working on too many

---

9 Council of Economic Advisers, *Annual Report 2009*, Tables B-46 and B-53. Available at www. gpoaccess.gov/eop/2009/2009_erp.pdf.

different things, and since we are not likely to be great at *all* of them, we will be poorer as a result. In the same way, even a developed economy such as that of the United States benefits from trade with other countries because it enables us to focus on what we do best and to exchange that output for what other countries can produce at a lower relative cost.

This is formally known as the law of comparative advantage. People, cities, states, and countries gain by specializing in activities that take best advantage of the talents and resources available to them and trading for what they do not produce themselves. This allows the world to produce more of everything that is needed. At least for the moment, a country like China can assemble lots of consumer goods—from my sandals to my laptop—more cheaply than we can in the United States. At the same time, with a better-educated workforce, we do lots of higher value, technology-intensive things more efficiently than developing countries. This includes designing innovative new products and physically producing aircraft, automobiles, chemical materials, and pharmaceuticals.

As countries like China develop, their citizens obtain higher levels of education, their financial markets function better, and their technological capabilities improve. This often changes their areas of comparative advantage so that productive resources are reallocated to more valuable pursuits, even if they have to suffer some unemployment in the process. As was discussed previously, this type of unemployment usually affects a relatively small portion of the population, and while challenging, it is not necessarily permanent. Since international trade increases the overall opportunities and wealth available to a country, it is possible to use some of those added resources to help newly unemployed workers obtain new skills.

China's transition from an isolated and impoverished nation to an open economy with access to world markets began in 1979. Taking a gradual approach, China's government opened one major coastal city at a time to trade with foreign countries, until the creative power of over one billion people was unleashed. Eventually, tens of millions of poor rural farmers began the difficult journey from west to east in hopes of finding a better life for themselves and their children. As the population poured into the coastal cities, a country and its people were completely transformed, and the world has been eagerly consuming the enormous number of products that resulted ever since.

Transforming China into a participant in a globally integrated economy has been challenging, and it remains an ongoing process. Some enormous tasks, such as establishing a competitive financial system, true property rights, and a balanced domestic economy with greater individual freedom, remain on China's to-do list. But for the woman I met in Guilin, the economy improved quickly enough that her parents could afford to take her younger siblings off the farm and send them to school. In 1980, the average Chinese person earned the inflation-adjusted equivalent of about $520 a year. By 2008, that number had risen to over $5,000.[10] In less than three decades, then, China's real per capita income rose almost tenfold.

Another measure of China's progress is provided by the World Bank, which classifies anyone in a developing country earning less than a $1.25 a day as officially poor. Using this standard, the World Bank determined that between 1981 and 2005 the incidence of rural poverty in China fell dramatically, from 84 percent to 16 percent of the population.[11] In only 24 years, approximately 628 million Chinese people escaped extreme poverty.

While China's still ongoing journey from poverty to prosperity is one of the most fascinating examples of the creative power of trade, we might be tempted to ask if their gains came at our expense. Percentagewise, the Chinese have gained enormously, and when you're starting from a base income of 10 dollars per person per week, even small increases in income will be life altering. But we haven't done badly ourselves. Over that 1980–2008 period, real per capita annual incomes in the United States rose from about $25,000 to over $40,000, an increase of 60 percent.[12]

That is part of why, when I look at the labels on my jeans or shoes or toothbrush or laptop, I don't get angry or resentful. When we trade with another country, rich or poor, we both gain. Our trading partners become a part of a global economy and eventually gain access to all of the investment, customers, employers, technology, and ideas that come with it. Sure, participating in international trade inevitably exposes a country to competition that can result in difficult transitions, such as the ones faced by my grandfather and father. Ultimately, though, such changes drive us closer to discovering what our greatest strengths really are.

No individual can be a "master of all trades," and neither can any group of individuals, be it a state or a country. Trade between people and groups is the best way to do more with the limited time, skills, and resources that we have. And if you limit peoples' capacity to trade with others, you are likely condemning them to a life of poverty. Before you assume that limits on trade are needed so that we can avoid even temporary displacement of workers, consider the one billion truly poor people, mostly concentrated around the equator, who do not have appropriate access to international markets and all of the food, technology, and education that it could eventually provide.

I started this chapter pointing out just a few of the countries that made my morning routine easy, efficient, and cheap, but now it's important to

---

10 World Bank Group, *World Development Indicators & Global Development Finance.* Available at http://databank.worldbank.org.

11 Ibid.

12 A concept called purchasing power parity (PPP) allows for international comparisons such as this. PPP can be used to calculate how much foreign currency would be needed to purchase goods in the United States. In this case, PPP methods are used to make comparisons in inflation-adjusted 2005 U.S. dollars.

stress something we all too often forget: Countries do not produce things—people do. When we see the "Made in" label on anything we enjoy, we should think of the individuals who used their time and talents to provide it for us. They may not be from Alabama or Michigan, but the *mutual* gains from trade do not disappear when it happens across a national border or between people of different races. Regardless of who is involved, trading freely with others is a peaceful and effective way to improve our lives. That's not something we should be angry about but rather something to celebrate.

READ ON/JOIN UP

➢ For all the data, facts, and theory needed to make someone think twice about throwing a Molotov cocktail in a fit of antitrade rage, check out:
   Irwin, Douglas. *Free Trade Under Fire*. Princeton, NJ: Princeton University Press, 2005.

➢ Just in case checking product labels does not have you convinced, see how many countries, governments, and people get involved in putting a simple T-shirt on your back:
   Rivoli, Pietra. *The Travels of a T-Shirt in the Global Economy: An Economist Examines the Markets, Power, and Politics of World Trade*. Hoboken, NJ: John Wiley & Sons, 2005.

➢ For a clear starting point on a wide variety of interesting topics concerning China, see:
   Naugton, Barry. *The Chinese Economy, Transitions and Growth*. Cambridge: Massachusetts Institute of Technology Press, 2007.

➢ For quick links to the Web sites discussed below, please visit *www.pearsonhighered.com/walters*.
   If you are interested in keeping track of which countries are embracing world trade and which ones are drifting toward isolation, head over to Global Trade Alert. This site provides real-time information on the new laws and policies that affect foreign trade and the countries involved. See how U.S. tax laws might favor domestic beer instead of foreign or how Turkey is making it easier to import wheat and sheep.

   For an excellent visual way of exploring loads of global trade data and plenty of other basic economic indicators, check out the Gapminder Foundation. The Web site's interactive graphs and free desktop application are a fun way to literally watch different countries evolve from the 1800s to the present right before your eyes.

QUESTIONS FOR DISCUSSION

1. It's common to hear about American firms "outsourcing" jobs to foreign countries. From the perspective of those countries, then, something called "insourcing" must be going on. Would it be possible for a country

to "insource" jobs without ever "outsourcing" any? If so, under what conditions? Based on Figure 1.1 in this chapter (or any other evidence you might gather), do you think America does any "insourcing"?

2. Adam Smith wrote in 1776 (in *The Wealth of Nations*) that the "effects of the division of labour, in the general business of society, will be more easily understood by considering in what manner it operates in some particular manufactures." What is "the division of labor"? To help understand it, choose one of your favorite possessions and consider (perhaps accompanied by a little research) all the people, companies, organizations, or countries that must have influenced its creation and delivery. How is this very old concept related to contemporary debates about globalization and trade?

3. This chapter raises the possibility that companies facing foreign or domestic competition could be "protected" from their rivals. How could this be done? What would the effects be on the protected firms' incentives to produce efficiently? On their customers' well-being?

4. My friends and I enjoy ranking and endlessly debating the order of our top 5 favorite movies, cars, bands, books, and so forth—or sometimes our bottom 5. See if you can find a world ranking of the countries most open to trade (in terms of the share of their national output that is either imports or exports, as Figure 1.1 shows for the United States). Also see if you can find the countries least open to trade by this measure. Based on what you can find out about life in these countries, do you have any preference about where you'd rather live?

5. The chapter points out that Chinese incomes have grown very rapidly (roughly tenfold) in recent decades, after adjusting for inflation. If wages keep rising in China, what will happen to its comparative advantage in low-cost manufacturing over time? How will that affect trade between the United States and China or other countries?

CHAPTER 2

The War on the Economy

Stimulus Spending and Job "Creation"

by Steven A. Maex

The essential act of war is destruction, not necessarily of human lives, but of the products of human labor.

—EMMANUEL GOLDSTEIN IN GEORGE ORWELL'S *1984*[1]

Chapter Highlights

- Opportunity Cost
- Economic Stimulus
- Business Cycles
- Gross Domestic Product
- The Keynesian Multiplier

Where were you on September 11, 2001? What memories do you carry from that fateful Tuesday morning?

I remember being kept mostly in the dark that day. In eighth grade at the time, my only suspicion that something was wrong came from a radio broadcast that I overheard in my computer class. I vividly remember the broadcaster declaring that a plane had struck the World Trade Center. Of course, this was only the beginning. My teachers—feeling they had to protect me and my classmates from the traumatic effects of the horrors occurring in New York, Washington, and a field in Pennsylvania—said as little as possible about the events. The atmosphere in our school was nevertheless tense. My religion teacher left the room for close to 10 minutes in the middle of class and returned in tears. When we asked her what was wrong, she simply responded, "Pray."

In the days that followed, newspapers, websites, and the airwaves, were filled with analyses of how "the world had changed." Some were angry, some thoughtful and reverent—and some presented a different perspective.

---

1 Orwell, George. *1984*. Ed. Erich Fromm. New York: Harcourt, 1949 .

Paul Krugman, the 2008 Nobel Prize winner in Economics, offered one of those different perspectives, writing, "Ghastly as it may seem to say this, the terror attack—like the original day of infamy, which brought an end to the Great Depression—could even do some economic good."[2]

Clearly, Krugman did not *want* war or terrorist attacks. His argument was that our *response* to those attacks likely would stimulate a sluggish economy. That is, he wasn't focused on the terrorist attacks themselves but on the expenditures to rebuild the World Trade Center and the "war on terror" that would inevitably follow those attacks. And on the surface, there appears to be some historic evidence to support this idea. Looking at the events of the 1930s and 1940s, one can conclude that World War II helped the United States' economy emerge from the depths of the Great Depression.

So, how does replacing destroyed buildings or funding a war effort stimulate the economy? It sure *seems* like jobs will be created. Construction workers are needed to rebuild structures, soldiers to fight, and factory workers to manufacture bombs and planes. That's where a lot of politicians, businessmen, and everyday Americans tend to focus—and even President George W. Bush accepted that logic. In a 2008 NBC interview, when asked about the economic impact of the war in Iraq, Bush posited, "I think, actually, that the spending on the war may help with jobs."[3] It's amazing that Mr. Bush and Mr. Krugman, who are typically on opposite ends of the political spectrum, both view destructive events in same economic light—as simulative to the economy.

Now, I never thought I would side with a 1970s Motown performer over a Nobel Prize winner on an economic issue. But in Edwin Starr's 1970 hit "War," he enthusiastically declared what war is good for: "Absolutely nuthin'!" To more accurately reflect this discussion, though, his answer can be modified slightly to, "Absolutely nuthin' *economically.*"[4]

Whether or not a particular war is necessary or proper can be debated on many criteria. Is it moral? Is it just? Does it make us more safe and secure? Yet the consensus has always been that, if nothing else, war is good for the economy. Unfortunately, this overlooks one of the most fundamental concepts in economics. Now, I'm not arguing against war in the general sense; I only hope to show that the so-called simulative impact of war should not be counted as a benefit or justification.

In this chapter, we look at the economic consequences of war from several angles, the first of which relates to property damage. To start to see how the "war as economic stimulus" argument might fall short, let's travel to the hypothetical town of Maynard City.

---

2 Krugman, Paul. "Reckonings; After the Horror." *New York Times*. April 19, 2009. Available at www.nytimes.com/2001/09/14/opinion/reckonings-after-the-horror.html.

3 Krugman, Paul. "Bush Is Right about Something." *New York Times*. February 19, 2008. Available at http://krugman.blogs.nytimes.com/2008/02/19/bush-is-right-about-something/.

4 Starr and I are probably on the same wavelength, but I do grant him that there aren't too many words that rhyme with "economically."

MAYNARD CITY: WHERE DESTRUCTION BRINGS PROSPERITY

One October afternoon, a man named Sam Jones was anxiously watching his big-screen TV as his beloved Maynard City Mud Dogs attempt to win their first World Series on the road in Baltimore.[5] One out away from victory in the climactic game, he was overcome with agony as O's All-Star catcher Matt Weiters hit a monstrous walk-off homerun that struck the B&O Warehouse over the Camden Yards flag court. In a violent fit of frustration, Mr. Jones grabbed a sledgehammer, walked outside, and began to obliterate everything in his path. He destroyed cars, mailboxes, windows, and even his neighbor's LCD television as it was being delivered by UPS.

After the police hauled Sam off to jail, he was contacted by a lawyer willing to defend him. His name was John Keynes III, the grandson of the world renowned economist for which Keynesian economics was named. He said that he had an airtight defense for Sam's actions, and once in court he argued passionately on Sam's behalf. Pointing to the pictures of the wreckage on display in the courtroom, John asked the judge, "How can you find this man guilty of damaging Maynard City? Don't you see all the jobs he created? He should not be thrown in jail but given a parade!" John's argument was that to replace all that Sam had broken, increased demand for autoworkers, window installers, and mailbox manufacturers was inevitable, and Maynard City would prosper as a result.

Surprisingly, though, the judge didn't buy John's defense. She said, a bit mysteriously, "Stop there! Your theory is confined to what is seen; it takes no account of that which is not seen."[6] Obviously well read, she was citing a principle known as the broken window fallacy, articulated by a 19-century economist named Frederic Bastiat. This fallacy applies when individuals erroneously believe, like John and Sam did, that destruction breeds prosperity due to the fact that resources must be spent and, in some cases, jobs created to repair all that was demolished.

However, in a nutshell, Sam's actions hindered rather than helped the economy because of what economists call opportunity cost—or "that which is not seen." To figure out the opportunity cost of any action you take, just think of what you're giving up as a result and what that foregone alternative might be worth. For example, when I chose to begin college full-time, in addition to paying for tuition, room and board, and books, I also gave up the ability to work full-time for four years. In this case, the salary that I would have made working is my opportunity cost. As you can imagine, opportunity costs are often overlooked because they are unseen—really, they're "what could have been."

The judge saw through John's argument and pointed out that Sam is not a hero. Rather than stimulating the local economy, Sam forced his

---

5 Okay, I'm an Orioles fan—my hypothetical example, my fantasy.

6 Bastiat, Frederic. "What Is Seen and What Is Not Seen." *Library of Economics and Liberty*. April 23, 2009. Available at www.econlib.org/library/Bastiat/basEss1.html.

neighbors to spend money simply to restore their previous standard of living. Their wealth decreased, they received nothing new in return, and, as a result, they'll likely be unable to go out and buy other products that they previously desired. Looks like Sam's neighbor, Bill, may have to say bye-bye to that gas fireplace he and his wife wanted. The money Bill would have used for the purchase is now needed to replace that which has been broken.

But Sam's neighbors must have had insurance, right? Phew! Thank goodness the sledgehammered property will be replaced after all, and for "free." Well, not so fast. Insurers collect premiums that they expect are sufficient to cover their costs, including payouts for damages, and profit for their shareholders. Unexpected payouts will inevitably force insurers to raise premiums, which will be spread over a larger group of insurance policyholders, some of whom had their property damaged and some who didn't. People who have never even met Sam would suffer losses because of his actions.

And what if Sam had *controlled* his temper? What could his neighbors have done with all the money they'll have to spend to return to their predestruction state or to cover the increased cost of their insurance premiums? Maybe they could've built a new deck, bought a new car, or even acquired a loveable Rottweiler that might dissuade hotheads like Sam from future acts of destruction. Even if they just socked the money away in a savings account, their bank could lend it to some other person or company who wants to spend it. In either case, society would be far better off overall if Sam had not gone on his rampage.

JOBS, BABY, JOBS!

While John's arguments for increased spending didn't help Sam that day, maybe the judge missed something when she dismissed John's ideas. In particular, does Bastiat's point about opportunity cost remain relevant when there are resources, people included, that are *not* currently being employed within the economy? What if there were lots of unemployed autoworkers and window installers sitting idle before Sam destroyed his neighborhood? They will certainly benefit from the new windows and cars that will be demanded, right?

Before addressing that question, it is important to understand why resources are idle in the first place. Their dormant state could stem from either of two overarching causes. First, the resources may not be demanded in their current form because consumers' tastes have changed or because new technology has enabled their tastes to be satisfied more cheaply. In these cases, the resources would be better employed elsewhere, helping to make things that people actually demand at a given price. Second, it might be attributable to a business cycle—for instance, a macroeconomic downturn that has caused income across the board to decrease and demand for a wide variety of resources to fall.[7] As a result, many resources that were employed in the past will become idle since there is no longer a demand for them, at least temporarily.

Regardless of their cause, economic meltdowns that lead to idle resources usually result in calls for more government spending to "prime the pump,"[8] increase demand for goods and services, and get the economy back on track. And while the idea of government spending to solve the economy's ills seems to differ from John's notion that destruction can contribute to greater prosperity, both stem from the same theory. Assuming there is "slack" in the economy, the argument here is that the spending to rebuild New York City after the terror attacks on September 11 and the spending that government engages in with the purpose of pump-priming both result in a similar economic end: employing otherwise idle resources, thus stimulating the economy. The idea was first posited by John Maynard Keynes back in the mid-1930s in his *General Theory*, during the worldwide Great Depression, and Keynesian theory soon became integrated into mainstream economic and political discourse.

What's more, in Keynes's view, the ultimate benefit of stimulus spending would be far greater than the initial outlay, since ripple effects would follow the initial burst of spending. Thus, even relatively small increases in expenditures can have a much larger effect on overall demand and output. That is, an initial increase in spending can have a *multiplied effect* on national income (measured in terms of gross domestic product, or GDP[9]), with the "Keynesian multiplier" equal to the extra amount of national income obtained per dollar of additional government spending.

To see how this multiplier might work, backtrack to September 11, 2001, and subsequent years. The initial spending to replace the fallen towers or repair the Pentagon employed steel manufacturers and other contractors; these manufacturers and contractors spent all or part of their income in other areas of economy; the recipients of that spending enjoyed higher incomes and spent elsewhere, and so on.

If, as most Keynesians assume, the multiplier is significantly greater than 1, we have some amazingly powerful medicine to treat economic

---

7 Of course, there's considerable debate about the causes of macroeconomic busts and booms. One theory that has received increasing attention since the financial crisis of 2007–2009 is the Austrian theory of the business cycle, which holds (among other things) that economic downturns are often a result of loose monetary policy that promotes excessive investment that, eventually, leads to a collapse. For more on this theory, see Thomas Woods's *Meltdown*, about which more information is provided in the Read On/Join Up section at the end of Chapter 9.

8 These days, old-fashioned water pumps are scarce, so I've never personally "primed" one. It just means you have to pour some water over it to create the vacuum that gets the pump started.

9 GDP refers to the market value of all final goods and services produced within a country over a given period of time. It is one measure of the performance of an economy, although it is considered by many to be imperfect due to the fact that, for example, it does not account for transactions that take place outside of organized markets (in "the underground economy").

illnesses. Want another $100 billion in GDP? Well, if the multiplier is 4, the government just needs to spend $25 billion, say, building roads. The construction workers will spend some or all of those dollars, the recipients will spend more, those beneficiaries will do the same, and incomes will continue to grow until the ripples fade and we have an extra $100 billion in GDP.

Unfortunately, however, things might not be that easy. In recent years, the size of the multiplier has become the subject of much debate among economists. When government wants to increase expenditures, it has to get the money by either raising taxes or borrowing. Since tax increases would reduce the amount that we consumers have available to spend and defeat the purpose of the government's spending, most Keynesians recommend just borrowing the money (i.e., "deficit spending"). But that might leave less borrowing available for businesses to tap when they want to expand their operations (and create jobs) or for us when we want to buy a new car or house.[10] The bottom line is that this sort of "crowding out" of private borrowing and spending by the government might really put a dent in the multiplier. If consumers look at all that new government borrowing and start saving more because we know our taxes are going way up when all that debt has to be repaid, then look out—the multiplier might get pretty close to 0. Also, if the government is spending money on projects consumers do not value, the pump-priming story starts to lose some appeal.

Robert Barro is one researcher who has concluded that government spending, especially in wartime, might be a "dampener, rather than a multiplier." During the debate over 2009 economic stimulus legislation signed by President Obama, Prof. Barro summarized his disagreement with Keynesian thinking by stating that "if this [multiplier] mechanism is genuine, one might ask why the government should stop with only $1 trillion of added purchases."[11]

Other economists are all over the map on this issue. For example, Valerie Ramey concluded that an extra dollar of government spending raises GDP by about $1.40, while Harald Uhlig found that the government spending multiplier gets smaller over time and is actually negative in the long run. On the other hand, Christina and David Romer have found that a dollar of tax cuts (which boost private rather than government spending)

---

10 It gets even more complicated once you start thinking about the rest of the world. If the extra government borrowing causes interest rates to go up, foreigners will want to lend us money; when they buy dollars so they can use them to buy the bonds the government is selling to finance its deficits, the dollar will get stronger, and that will hurt our export industries—again partially defeating the purpose of the pump-priming. Told you this stimulus thing isn't as easy as it looks.

11 Barro, Robert J. "Government Spending Is No Free Lunch." *Wall Street Journal.* January 22, 2009, p. A17. Last accessed September 25, 2010, at http://online.wsj.com/article/SB123258618204604599.html.

can boost GDP by about 3 dollars.[12] Why all the disagreement? It's hard to isolate the effect a change in one aspect of the economy when so many other things are changing simultaneously. That said, let's see what we can learn by taking a closer look at the most popular example cited as proof that war is "good for the economy."

WORLD WAR II: THE GREAT EMPLOYMENT PROGRAM

The Great Depression was an awful economic period in the United States. And on the surface, it appears that the United States emerged from it just as Keynes would have expected: with the huge boost in government spending that accompanied World War II. Thousands of unemployed individuals were put to work in the war effort, and the demand for numerous other resources—such as those used for building armaments—allowed their producers to thrive. On closer examination, though, we'll see that wartime spending, though certainly militarily necessary, actually slowed the United States' recovery from the Great Depression.

The root cause of the Depression is another macroeconomic topic that generates many differences of opinion.[13] Many blame excessively tight monetary policy that began in 1928. Many point to the wealth losses resulting from the stock market crash in 1929. Still others point to policy blunders such as the Smoot-Hawley Tariff, which raised taxes on U.S. imports to an average of 59.1 percent.[14] But there's no disagreement about the severity of the meltdown: From 1929 to 1933, inflation-adjusted GDP fell by over 26 percent,[15] and the unemployment rate[16] rose from 3 to 25 percent.[17] These job losses led to poverty on a grand scale that left very few unaffected.

---

12 For a useful short summary of this issue, see: U.S. Senate Joint Economic Committee. "Keynesian Tax and Spending Multipliers." February 2, 2009. Available at http://jec.senate.gov/republicans/public/index.

13 There's an old joke that "if you laid all the economists in the world end to end...they'd all point in different directions."

14 This, of course, set off a firestorm of retaliation in which countries around the world began to impose similar tariffs on products produced in the United States and exported abroad. See DiLorenzo, Thomas J. *How Capitalism Saved America.* New York: Three Rivers, 2004, p. 172.

15 Bureau of Economic Analysis. "Current Dollar and 'Real' Gross Domestic Product." November 6, 2010. Available at www.bea.gov/national/xls/gdplev.xls.

16 The unemployment rate is the percentage of the labor force actively pursuing employment but unable to find it. According to the Bureau of Labor Statistics, unemployed persons are "all persons who had no employment during the reference week, were available for work, except for temporary illness, and had made specific efforts to find employment sometime during the 4-week period ending with the reference week. Persons who were waiting to be recalled to a job from which they had been laid off need not have been looking for work to be classified as unemployed." See www.bls.gov/dolfaq/bls_ques23.htm.

17 U.S. Bureau of Labor Statistics. "Compensation from before World War I through the Great Depression." November 6, 2010. Available at www.bls.gov/opub/cwc/cm20030124ar03p1.htm#37a.

But starting in 1933, the U.S. economy began a strong recovery. Even with a recessionary blip in 1937 and 1938, the average rate of growth of real GDP from 1933 to 1940 was over 8 percent a year, almost three times the long-term average real growth rate. In fact, by the time the United States entered World War II at the end of 1941, GDP had recovered to its pre-Depression level and the unemployment rate had fallen below 10 percent.[18] Clearly, then, the U.S. economy didn't wait for WWII to get it moving in the right direction; for all that the war effort did to save the world from fascist domination, the stimulative effect of wartime spending has been greatly exaggerated in the history books.

It is true that real (inflation-adjusted) GDP grew by over 70 percent[19] between 1940 and 1945, and official unemployment fell to an incredibly low 1.3 percent by 1944.[20] Workers who had been idle (as well as some engaged in productive work that just didn't happen to be included in government statistics) were counted as officially employed during the war effort. But what we have to remember is that these workers also could have performed *other* tasks. The resources used to defeat the Axis powers were diverted from their other areas of the economy. Both Keynesians and non-Keynesians likely wished WWII hadn't happened, because then all that wartime spending could have been used to stimulate further recovery via funding for important infrastructure projects, new community parks, or more scientific research. Or, alternatively, tax cuts or less government borrowing could have allowed Americans to spend more of their hard-earned money on things they valued, fueling continued recovery.

That incredibly low wartime unemployment rate reflects this diversion of resources, and the chart on the next page illustrates the tradeoff that occurred.[21] In 1940, 82.4 percent of U.S. workers were employed in nondefense occupations, 1.8 percent were in defense-related jobs, and the rest—15.7 percent—were officially unemployed.[22] By 1944, nondefense employment had fallen to 58.4 percent of the labor force, defense-related jobs had risen to 40.3 percent, and unemployment was at the aforementioned 1.3 percent.[23] So defense-sector employment rose by more than

---

18 That's after adjusting the official rate for the fact that the government counted all those in emergency employment programs as unemployed. See Darby, Michael R. "Three-and-a-Half Million U.S. Employees Have Been Mislaid: Or, an Explanation of Unemployment, 1934–1941." *Journal of Political Economy*, 84 (February 1976), pp. 1–16.

19 Bureau of Economic Analysis. "Current Dollar and 'Real' Gross Domestic Product." November 6, 2010. Available at www.bea.gov/national/xls/gdplev.xls.

20 U.S. Bureau of Labor Statistics. "Employment Status of the Civilian Noninstitutional Population, 1940 to Date." April 19, 2009. Available at www.bls.gov/cps/cpsaat1.pdf.

21 Higgs, Robert. "Wartime Prosperity? A Reassessment of the U.S. Economy in the 1940s." *The Independent Review*. April 20, 2009. Available at www.independent.org/newsroom/article.asp?id=138.

22 Remember, though, that if you were in an emergency program you were officially *unemployed*; see footnote 17.

23 Higgs. "Wartime Prosperity?"

Figure 2.1 U.S. Employment, Fiscal Years 1940–1947

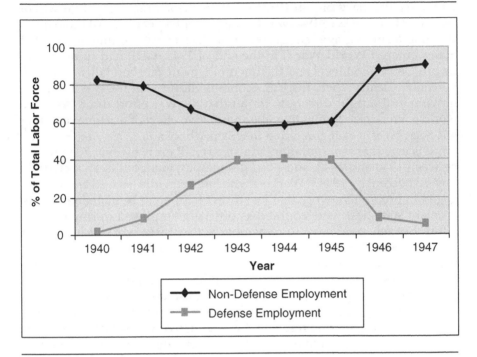

Source: Author created based on data from the article Higgs, Robert. "Wartime Prosperity? A Reassessment of the U.S. Economy in the 1940s." *The Independent Review*. April 20, 2009. Available at www.independent.org/newsroom/article.asp?id=138.

unemployment fell, meaning that the war effort did not merely sop up unemployed resources but diverted many employed civilians into military and defense occupations, which is opportunity cost in a nutshell. Even though the war effort helped end the Holocaust and the Axis dreams of world domination, it also prevented the employed from contributing to the betterment of the lives of ordinary Americans in their civilian occupations.[24]

To recap, there are two major problems with claims that World War II "cured" the Great Depression. First, GDP and unemployment data from the period indicate that the recovery was well underway before the attack on Pearl Harbor. Second, once the United States entered the war, valuable resources, including employable young men and women, were diverted from producing goods of benefit to the average American into the production of material necessary to fight the war.

More generally, when there's a dark cloud overhead—an act of terrorism or a natural disaster—and you hear some pundit suggest that it

24 Ibid.

might contain an economic silver lining and that jobs might be created as a result, just shake your head and know that that person, no matter how smart or famous, has taken no account of "that which is not seen."

READ ON/JOIN UP

➤ For a well-researched and comprehensive argument against the concept of wartime "prosperity," see:
    Higgs, Robert. *Depression, War, and Cold War: Challenging the Myths of Conflict and Prosperity.* Oakland, CA: Independent Institute, 2006.

➤ For more information on the implications and repercussions of the Great Depression, and the government's response to it, see:
    Shlaes, Amity. *The Forgotten Man: A New History of the Great Depression.* New York: HarperCollins, 2007.

➤ For a quick link to the Web site regarding the topic below, please visit *www.pearsonhighered.com/walters*:
    For a continuous discussion around the free-market economic concepts made famous by one of the men at the heart of this chapter, Frederic Bastiat, see the Bastiat Society.

QUESTIONS FOR DISCUSSION

1. Think about the most expensive thing you bought within the last year. Compile a list of the things you could have bought instead with roughly the same amount of money. Did you consider these alternatives at the time you made the transaction in question? That is, when you buy things, do you think only of their money price, or do you translate that into "opportunities foregone"? Why or why not?

2. The chapter notes that there is a lot of debate as to how business cycles—especially recessions or depressions—get started. Perform a little research and identify at least three commonly cited causes for the Great Depression of the 1930s.

3. If a government borrows money to spend it on things it believes will stimulate the economy, some economists fear there will be "crowding out" of private spending. How could this happen? Are there conditions in which this "crowding-out effect" might be more (or less) likely?

4. Many have drawn parallels between the economic collapse of 2007–2009 and the Great Depression. What similarities and differences do you see, particularly regarding the part that wartime expenditures played during these trying times? (Hint: Make sure you consider when the wars occurred, and think of opportunity cost.)

5. According to the chapter, there is a great deal of disagreement among economists about exactly how strong the Keynesian multiplier actually is in practice. Why do you think this is so hard to pin down precisely—unlike, say, measuring the speed of sound or determining the appropriate dose of antibiotic to cure an infection? If you were an economic researcher, what kind of experiment might you like to conduct to address this issue?

CHAPTER 3

(Don't) Give Us Your Tired, Your Poor . . .

Labor Migration in the Land of the Free and Beyond

by Daniel G. O'Neill

> *You live in the age of interdependence. Borders don't count for much or stop much, good or bad, anymore.*
>
> —BILL CLINTON

Chapter Highlights

- Immigration Policy
- Economic Growth
- Unemployment
- Aggregate Demand and Supply
- Marginal Revenue Product of Labor

My train was just about to leave Madrid. As I ran from the Metro into Atocha station, the departures board told me I didn't have much time. I was headed to my apartment in Alcalá de Henares, a neighboring town. Missing this train would add an extra hour to my journey home.

Dodging the inbound travelers on the platform, I slid through the doors of my train just before they closed and found a seat across from a young couple. Relieved, I popped in my headphones and gazed out the window as we pulled away from the station. It was late afternoon, about siesta time, but an international student like me was much more interested in soaking in the sights than napping.

I had been depending on and enjoying Spain's public transportation system for several weeks now. There was always a mixture of travelers on the train, so people-watching was a great way to occupy the time. I looked around the car.

An old woman carrying the day's groceries. Pretty typical. A businessman in a sharp suit, deep in conversation on his cell phone. A young mother juggling a loaf of bread in one arm and an infant in the other. A teenage rebel with his lip pierced, his techno music audible even over my own iPod and the train's rumbling.

Most passengers were easily identifiable as Spanish natives. With my pale Irish skin and less-than-Castilian Spanish accent, I was a rare exception. But as we got farther from the city, I noticed that many of those who boarded had even darker skin than a typical Spaniard. These men wore tattered flannel shirts and dirty blue jeans, some carrying six-packs of San Miguel beer. They were clearly heading home after a day of manual labor.

I couldn't quite place these men in the same category as the Spaniards, so when I got back to my apartment, I mentioned them to my roommate, Pablo, who confirmed my suspicions. Many of the workers on the train probably weren't Spanish at all but were most likely immigrants who had come to Spain to work in the booming construction industry.

As it turns out, when there is work to be done, Spain isn't all that different from the United States. It tends to hire cheap immigrant laborers with a good work ethic and the desire to make a decent living. It just so happens that a lot of those workers are Moroccan instead of Mexican.

Before studying in Spain, I was aware that a lot of Americans complained about Mexicans and other immigrants entering the United States, especially when they arrived illegally or took American jobs. After seeing an abundance of working-class foreigners in Spain during my four months there, I came to the conclusion that Spain had as much of an immigrant problem as the United States did. But I didn't hear any Spaniards complaining about it. Where were the gripes against immigrants that I had become familiar with in America?

After a bit of research, I learned that many of Spain's immigrants had originally entered the country illegally. But, starting in the late 1990s, Spain began to drastically reform its immigration policies and open its borders. Along the coast, undocumented immigrants found little opposition from Spanish authorities. Inland, amnesty programs granted hundreds of thousands of immigrants legal residency. Basically, Spain just stopped calling many of its immigrants illegal, and they became vital contributors to the economy. And, at least from where I stood, it didn't seem all that bad.

It got me to thinking. What would happen if the United States threw open its borders? Would unemployment skyrocket as Mexicans, Indians, and Chinese rushed to take all our jobs? Would the poverty rate soar as cities overflowed with people?

It would be nice if we could try it out for a few months, just to see what happened. If we didn't like what we saw, we could hit the "undo" button and revert. But so far, no one has figured out an easy way to take freer immigration for a U.S. test run. I guess the next best thing is to look at a place, like Spain, that has already given it a shot.

SPAIN'S BIG IDEA

Spain is in a unique position in Europe. Its southern tip is less than 10 miles from Morocco and the rest of North Africa. The Strait of Gibraltar is the only thing separating one continent from the other. When I visited Morocco, the 45 minutes it took to cross the narrow strait turned my ferry into a portal between two worlds.

The streets of Tangier were crowded with Moroccans in traditional Islamic robes. Merchants sold dates and North African spices at the bazaar. Street signs written in Arabic dotted the narrow alleys and dirt roads. Decorative tiles adorned most surfaces—floors, ceilings, walls. The differences between Spain and Morocco were astounding. And it appeared that many potential migrants, when given the choice between these two worlds, were choosing Spain.

For most of the twentieth century, Spain's population fled to the Americas or other parts of Europe. In migration terms, it was a "sending country," thanks to a civil war and general political instability. But by the 1980s, changes in the political climate had boosted Spain's international image, turning it into a "receiving country" and a gateway for immigrants into Europe. Much like Mexicans and other Latin Americans traveling north to be a part of the prosperity of the United States, many North Africans long to reach the shores of Spain, where Europe awaits with its long history of affluence.

During the 1980s, when immigrants began to arrive in larger numbers, Spain tried hard to keep them out. The country was scheduled to join the European Community (now the European Union) in 1986, and it had to meet the EC's standards for immigration. To do so, it put some harsh restrictions in place, like requiring migrants to have an existing job offer in Spain before they would be allowed in the country. The Spanish government saw immigration as a short-term problem that it needed to solve.

It was around a decade later that Spain realized its immigration "problem" wasn't going away. Attempts to crack down on illegal immigrants just led to an underground economy—a black market of undocumented workers. Sounds a lot like the situation faced by the United States. But the Spanish government gradually changed its attitude, realizing that illegal immigration was permanent and unavoidable, regardless of how hard they tried to stop it.

Around the turn of the millennium, Spain adopted two main immigration reforms.[1] These changes reflected a new outlook on immigration,

---

1 There were a lot of reforms occurring in Spain at this time, but the two most important for immigration were known as Law 4/2000 and the Greco Plan. Law 4/2000 defined the political and social rights of immigrants that came from non-EU countries. The measure was supported by three of the four major political parties in Spain and was a big step in the shift from a "temporary" view of immigration to a "permanent" view. The Greco Plan took things a step further by acknowledging that immigration could actually be beneficial to Spain if immigrants were integrated properly with Spanish society. The plan charged local and regional governments with the task of creating effective integration policies, like family reunification assistance, for example. The Greco Plan benefitted both EU and non-EU immigrants as well as refugees and displaced persons.

viewing it not as a problem but as an opportunity. Instead of treating immigrants as criminals, the government encouraged them to integrate with the Spanish culture and economy. This aimed to turn them into active contributors that could help Spain grow.

To encourage integration, the Spanish government has organized four amnesty programs since 1996, giving undocumented immigrants legal residency in the country. Many of the illegal immigrants who were granted amnesty had already been working in Spanish black market. The only thing that changed for them was their status as "illegal."

They continued to work, but now they were working in legitimate jobs for legitimate pay and the Spanish government was suddenly collecting taxes on their income. Employers found it harder to exploit their legal workers; they could no longer use an employee's illegal status as leverage to pay them low wages. In addition, the government didn't have to waste law enforcement dollars apprehending illegal workers, and the immigrants didn't have to worry about being sent back to their homelands.

It all sounds good, but did it actually work?

The performance of Spain's economy in recent decades indicates that increased immigration is correlated with economic growth—although, of course, correlation is not causality. From 1991 to 1997, before the reforms, real GDP growth in Spain averaged about 2 percent per year. In 1998, 57,000 immigrants arrived, and that number steadily increased until 2007, when over 600,000 immigrants were welcomed to the country.[2] During that same 10-year time period, real GDP growth jumped to between 3.5 and 4 percent annually, a major improvement.[3]

So the evidence suggests that increased immigration goes hand in hand with economic growth. What is unclear is the causality. Does increased immigration lead to economic growth? Or, does the presence of economic growth attract more immigrants? The answer is likely both.

Consider that the new millennium brought with it a housing boom (some would say "bubble"), with rapidly rising home prices and a flurry of new construction. As in the United States, Spain's construction industry was a driver of growth for the entire Spanish economy. It's inaccurate to say that immigrants were the chief cause of this economic growth, but they definitely enhanced it. You can't build new houses unless you have workers willing to do the job, and much of the new construction in Spain was performed by immigrant hands.

As this growth accelerated, eager immigrants arrived in Spain in larger numbers. They jumped at the chance to contribute to Spain's economy and were rewarded with jobs at attractive wages. Meanwhile, their

2 Matlack, Carol. "Spain: Immigrants Welcome." *Business Week Online*. May 21, 2007. Accessed November 13, 2010, at www.businessweek.com/magazine/content/07_21/b4035066.htm.

3 World Bank Group. *World Bank Data Catalog*. November 13, 2010. http://data.worldbank.org/country/spain.

contributions helped the economy grow even more, which in turn attracted more immigrants. As this "virtuous cycle" went on, unemployment, which had averaged 20.2 percent from 1990 to 1998, dropped all the way to 8 percent by 2007.[4]

It's worth noting that with the global financial meltdown that started in 2008, Spain's housing bubble burst and took much of the nation's economic growth with it. Real GDP growth turned negative and unemployment shot back up to 20 percent. As a result, immigration inflows to Spain decreased significantly, and some foreigners even began to "reverse migrate" back to their homelands. The foreign-born population of Spain grew only 1 percent in 2009, contrasted with the 17 percent growth of that group in 2007, at the peak of Spain's immigration rush.[5]

Evidently, during the recession, some immigrants saw more value in returning to their native countries than in struggling along with Spain's economy. But the housing boom provides a good example of how immigrants can be readily integrated into society when given the chance.

It also shows how immigration patterns respond to changes in the economy, and especially to the availability of jobs. Of course, people migrate for countless reasons besides employment. This has a lot of direct and indirect economic implications—some good and some bad. For example, national security concerns are some of the biggest noneconomic objections to immigration (especially illegal immigration) in today's world. Policymakers must also consider the impact that immigration has on education and healthcare, potential strains on the welfare system, cultural and language barriers, and a thousand other factors.[6]

We can't ignore the secondary or social impacts of immigration, but in this chapter we focus on immigrants as potential workers, which a great many of them are. So when we talk about the consequences of immigration, what we're really looking at is the economics of *labor migration*, and especially how that will affect "receiving" countries.

---

4 International Monetary Fund. "Spain Unemployment Rate." Accessed November 13, 2010, at www.indexmundi.com/spain/unemployment_rate.html.

5 Moffett, Matt, and House, Jonathan. "Spanish Downturn Sparks Immigrant Exodus." *Wall Street Journal*. July 1, 2010. Accessed November 13, 2010, at http://online.wsj.com/article/SB1 0001424052748703900004575325264137178190.html?mod=WSJ_business_EuropeNewsBucket.

6 The net impact of immigration on tax revenue has been frequently researched, weighing the gains (like additional taxes paid) versus the costs (such as welfare payments and other benefits received by immigrants). Studies have been done by the Center for Immigration Studies, the National Research Council, FAIR, the Heritage Foundation, the Pew Hispanic Center, the Perryman Group, and the American Immigration Council, just to name a few. The results vary, with some studies finding immigration to be a net cost to overall social welfare and others claiming it to have a net benefit. Whether positive or negative, the net impact is usually relatively close to zero.

PIZZA AND THE ECONOMY

But let's back up for a minute. We saw that the unemployment rate in Spain went *down* during a time when more immigrants were arriving, and it went *up* when immigration slowed to a trickle. How can this be? If new immigrants were taking Spanish jobs, wouldn't there be more unemployed Spaniards as more immigrants arrived, and vice versa?

To properly deal with these questions, we need to take another step back and rethink the way we look at the economy. Imagine that the economy is a giant pizza pie. There is a misconception that we're slicing up a pizza of a fixed size, with everyone getting smaller slices when someone new arrives at the table. But when more people choose to participate in the economy, the pizza gets bigger.

Bigger, because even though immigrants are sitting down at the table to eat, they are also bringing more ingredients to add to the pizza. These ingredients are things like technical skills and a strong work ethic, with which they can produce the goods and services that are needed in the economy. In economic terms, they add to the overall (aggregate) supply of labor, which allows more stuff to be produced.

When immigrants work and produce, they add value to an economy and enhance its growth. In general, the value they add is even *greater* than the wages that they command, since an employer wouldn't stay in business very long if she paid her workers more in wages than they generated in revenue for her business. Wages will always be less than or equal to a worker's "marginal revenue product"—the amount of additional revenue the firm earns as a result of the worker's contribution to output.

At the same time that immigrants are adding to the supply of goods and services by working, they are also participating in the economy as active consumers. Immigration, both legal and illegal, increases aggregate demand for things like housing, transportation, kitchen appliances, and medical attention. In a free economy, the amount of goods we produce and consume is not fixed, and neither is the number of jobs required to produce them. As immigrants produce, they earn; as they earn, they spend, and their spending will fuel job creation elsewhere in the economy.

So if immigrants add significant value to the economy, why do we restrict inflows of labor (and why do many advocate even tighter restrictions than we have now)? One popular answer is that we limit labor migration to protect jobs. When low-skilled immigrants arrive in the United States, they compete for jobs with low-skilled American workers and may be willing to work for lower wages. The upside is that this reduces the cost of producing various goods and services, which can benefit consumers in the form of lower prices in a competitive environment.

But there's potential downside, too—at least in the short run. Domestic workers face additional competition for their jobs as the supply of labor increases, which may drive down their wages or lead to unemployment.

Of course, many will find that, over time, their lost income or jobs can be restored in the sectors that expand as a result of immigrants' new demands for goods and services. Clearly, though, displaced workers will feel like they are getting a smaller slice of the pizza, and it will be difficult to console them with the "bigger pie" argument. This is why calls to restrict immigration flows to "protect" jobs are politically popular even though these restrictions may hurt the rest of society.

The potential short-term losses and painful transitions that some domestic workers face as a result of labor migration are real, but there are ways to ease this suffering. Since society as a whole has been made better off by the arrival of the new workers—with more output, lower prices, and more wealth—we should have the resources to pay for a properly constructed support system offering temporary unemployment benefits or retraining programs. This way, we can take advantage of all the benefits of immigration, while minimizing the amount of people who are worse off as a result of more open borders.

Everybody ♥ NY

Another way to see the benefits of opening a border is to look at the consequences of closing one.

Imagine that New Yorkers decide they don't like competing with all the sharp college graduates who move to the Big Apple and seek fame and fortune on Broadway, Wall Street, or Madison Avenue. So they get their elected officials to pass a law prohibiting any outsiders, whether from Connecticut or California, from moving to the Empire State and taking New Yorkers' jobs.

This kind of law is probably unconstitutional, but putting legal issues aside, it could be very politically attractive in New York. A theater major in Iowa or a marketing major in Wisconsin might object that such a law is going to kill his career plans, but he isn't going to vote in the New York elections, so it is a moot point, politically.

At first (in the short run), New Yorkers think this new law is great. The supply of workers, from actors to brokers and ad copy writers to Starbucks baristas, is now limited to those lucky enough to have been in-state before the "immigration wall" went up. This means the competition for those jobs is drastically reduced. Workers now have a lot of leverage, and they immediately start demanding higher wages. Since employers can't hire from out of state, they have little choice but to give in to the workers' demands.

Higher wages are generally good for employees but put New York employers in a tough spot. Since their production costs are higher, they are tempted to raise prices, putting them at a disadvantage when compared to firms in other states that get to hire in more competitive labor markets. If employers don't raise prices, the higher costs reduce profits, which means investors will start putting their money elsewhere and New York firms won't be able to expand, invest in new technology, or otherwise compete effectively. Existing New York companies will be held back by these high wages, grow more slowly, or even start to shrink.

Then think about the businesses that don't exist yet. New Yorkers are creative. They're thinking up new products or inventive ways of producing existing products all the time. Usually, that kind of innovation generates new job opportunities. In New York, however, with the new law prohibiting "outsiders" from taking those jobs, innovators will probably start taking their ideas elsewhere, and New Yorkers will miss out on all the good things that "foreigners" could have brought them. Without that influx of young actors from Iowa, maybe "off-Broadway" will mean "L.A." Or maybe the best new ad campaigns will be done in Madison, Wisconsin, instead of Madison Avenue.

In sum, it probably won't take long for New York's closed-border policy to start causing problems for its economy. Then things get interesting. A desperate Wall Street brokerage firm sneaks some ambitious Harvard Business School grads into town, teaches them how to speak with a New York accent, and puts them to work. Over time, the newspapers are full of exposés about how scams like this allow "undocumented workers" to steal New Yorkers' jobs.

It all sounds absurd, right? If any U.S. state closed its borders with the other 49, it would be foolish. There would be economic damage on *both* sides of that barrier. If that's the case, why don't we see that the same principles apply internationally? Shutting off labor migration between the Mexican state of Sonora and the U.S. state of Arizona isn't much different, economically at least, from building a wall between Arizona and Utah. The Founding Fathers understood this. At the Constitutional Convention in 1787, James Madison said, "That part of America which has encouraged the foreigner most has advanced the most rapidly in population, agriculture, and the arts."[7]

IMMIGRATION IS THE SINCEREST FORM OF FLATTERY

Like most choices in life, deciding whether to migrate or not forces a person to evaluate some tough tradeoffs. Whether in Morocco, Mexico, or anywhere else, potential immigrants ask the same question: *Based on my age, skills, family status, and so on, would I rather stay in my homeland to live and work, or should I risk emigrating?* They'll move only if the expected benefits outweigh the costs.

---

7 As quoted by Simon, Julian L., and James Simon, Rita. "Do We Really Need All These Immigrants?" in McCloskey, Donald N., ed., *Second Thoughts: Myths and Morals of U.S. Economic History* (2nd ed.). New York: Oxford University Press, 1993, p. 19.

This means, first, that immigrants generally have something valuable to offer, whether that's an able body and a strong work ethic or more formal, technical training. Second, they believe that their skills are likely to have a significantly higher payoff in their new country than in their old one, because any economic benefits they'll enjoy have to make up for the inherent costs of leaving their homeland and finding their way in a new culture. And since workers are generally paid no more than they contribute to their employers' revenues, we can infer that the payoffs to the firms that employ immigrants are greater still.

It's a myth that immigrants supply only low-skilled labor. Quite often, immigrants solve labor shortages in high-skilled occupations. Even as far back as the early 1980s, 26 percent of recent immigrants were professional and technical workers, versus 16 percent of native-born Americans.[8] But even when immigrants compete with Americans for low-skilled jobs—potentially reducing wages in these occupations—there are some long-term benefits for the economy, as we've seen. If wages and production costs fall, competition is likely to force firms to reduce prices, increasing consumers' spending power and the quantity of goods and services they can afford. That will cause firms to expand output, generating more job opportunities, and increasing social wealth—like Spain's "virtuous cycle."

Of course, there are a lot of factors that will affect peoples' decisions to emigrate or stay put: economic and social conditions in their homeland, transportation costs, legal constraints, preferences. But, as we've seen, a main factor will be the availability of jobs in the destination country. Living as an immigrant in a strange land will be much more appealing when there's work to be done, like during the housing booms in the United States and Spain. Likewise, a slow labor market will deter immigration. During the recent recession, it became clear that many illegal immigrants would rather not take the risks associated with emigrating to America. Inflows of undocumented foreigners, which had averaged 850,000 per year between 2000 and 2005, fell to 300,000 per year over 2007 to 2009.[9]

But that's exactly what you'd like to happen: When there is a shortage of labor in the destination country, resources should flow where they're needed. When there is a surplus of labor, the flow should taper off, or go the other way. So immigrants seem to be making rational economic decisions. And, when you think about it, immigrants' desire to participate in a destination country's economy is something of a compliment to that

---

8 Ibid., p. 22. It's easy to see why the myth is believed so widely, though. After all, we've all heard that poem that's inscribed at the base of the Statue of Liberty and which inspired the title of this chapter—all about how immigrants are "wretched refuse" and "huddled masses yearning to breathe free." Maybe we should add a verse about "skilled surgeons willing to save lives" or "brilliant engineers eager to build bridges."

9 Passel, Jeffrey S., and Cohn, D'Vera. "U.S. Unauthorized Immigration Flows Are Down Sharply Since Mid-Decade." September 1, 2010. Accessed November 13, 2010, at http://pewhispanic.org/files/reports/126.pdf.

country. It indicates that a nation's economy is perceived as strong and offers immigrants the opportunity to contribute to further growth. Allowing them to do so can start up a virtuous cycle and increase social wealth.

PEOPLE ARE NOT THE PROBLEM

You've probably heard the United States called a "melting pot." This just means that people from all over the world have come together to form one nation. Look back far enough, and you'll find that we're all the descendents of immigrants.[10]

Spain is a melting pot, too. Centuries of immigration have created a Spanish identity and culture that has been influenced by Celts, Romans, North African Muslims, Jews, and Latin Americans. And Spain's most prosperous times were those periods when immigrants were welcomed and everyone was allowed to coexist in peace.

For example, in the 15th century, the economy of the Spanish Empire suffered immensely when the "Catholic Kings" attempted to kick out all Jews and Muslims to make the Iberian Peninsula more culturally and religiously homogenous.[11] Many Muslims, known as "Moriscos," performed manual labor, often as farmers in the countryside, during a period when Christian society was rapidly becoming more educated and largely concentrating itself in cities. Historically restricted from owning land, Jews gravitated toward urban professions that were undesirable to Christians, such as tax collecting and banking (as Catholics were forbidden from lending money for interest at the time).

In 1492, the same year Columbus was discovering the New World, Ferdinand and Isabella were expelling the Jews from Spain, and the Moriscos soon after.[12] While the Spanish Empire survived, its economy was handicapped. Many jobs that required special skills went unfilled, and some educated city dwellers had to move back to the countryside and become farmers to replace the departed laborers. It was a major step back for the Spanish economy, which had been stronger and richer with the contributions of its immigrants than without them. We should expect a similar result if we kick immigrants out of the United States.

Although a mass expulsion of any group of immigrants is an extreme proposal, some claim it would give jobs back to Americans. There is surely some truth to that argument in the short run, just like some

---

10 Even Native Americans migrated from somewhere else, most likely via a land bridge over what is now the Bering Strait starting as far back as 30,000 years ago. So, immigration has a long history in this country.

11 Cantarino, Vicente. *Civilización y cultura de España*. Upper Saddle River, NJ: Pearson Prentice Hall, 2006.

12 Both groups were given the choice between expulsion and conversion to Catholicism. A portion chose to convert, while some maintained their religion in secret and others were forced out of Spain.

unemployed Spaniards in the 15th century may have welcomed the manual labor jobs that were freed up when the Moriscos left Spain. But in the long run, an economy is damaged when there are limits placed on those who can participate in it.

Prohibiting or limiting immigration ignores the benefits and opportunities immigrants create. Those who favor such policies tend to see the arrival of more people as a problem, when, in fact, people are much more likely to be a solution. Instead of looking at immigrants as a burden or as rivals for a piece of a "pie" of a fixed size, we've got to start thinking more about what they bring to the table. Throughout American history, immigrants have helped make us the economically and culturally rich nation we are today, and they're likely to continue to do so—as long as we let them.

READ ON/JOIN UP

➤ Much of modern thinking about the economic impact of immigration has been shaped and influenced by George Borjas. He has written various books and papers on the subject, but to get a good foundation in the facts, figures, and trends that matter, see:

Borjas, George J. "The Economics of Immigration." *Journal of Economic Literature*, 1994, vol. 32, no. 4, pp. 1667–1717.

➤ For a slightly more focused (and recent) look at the impact immigration has on wage levels in the United States, see:

Shapiro, Robert J., and Velluci, Jiwon. *The Impact of Immigration and Immigration Reform on the Wages of American Workers*. Washington, DC: New Policy Institute, 2010.

➤ If you want to hear the view of an Indian immigrant (and highly respected economist) on immigration, international trade, and a host of other economic issues, read:

Bhagwati, Jagdish. *In Defense of Globalization*. New York: Oxford University Press, 2004.

➤ For a quick link to the Web site regarding the topic below, please visit *www.pearsonhighered.com/walters*:

Immigration policy and potential reform is always a hot topic in American politics. To keep up with the latest ideas, proposals, and legislation, check out the Immigration Policy Center from the American Immigration Council. There's also a good resource page that will point you toward more research and articles about the economic impact of immigration.

QUESTIONS FOR DISCUSSION

1. Whenever my roommates and I have a cookout, we invite our friends and tell them to bring something to contribute to the feast. They can eat our food and drink our beer, but only if they add to the stockpile

of ground beef and sausage links that we have in the fridge. (a) What impact do you think these cookout "immigrants" have on the size, quality, and variety of the barbecue? Do you think this parallels the labor migration effects discussed in this chapter? (b) How does your answer change if a couple of friends *don't* contribute a dish? Or what if they only bring things my other friends don't attach much value to, like veggie burgers? (c) Can you think of any unintended consequences (or "secondary effects") of inviting more people to join the party (or economy)?

2. This chapter focused on economic issues related to immigration policy—e.g., effects on growth, unemployment, and wage rates. What noneconomic considerations must also be factored into decisions about immigration policy? Historically, how have societies like that of the United States (or any other with which you're familiar) addressed such considerations?

3. This chapter's example of New York creating a "barrier to entry" by workers from other states may seem unrealistic, but (historically) states have, in fact, tried to limit entry by those who wanted to sell things other than labor across state lines. Do a bit of research to identify situations where that has happened in the past. What were the key outcomes of such policies? What laws or institutions prevent that from happening these days?

4. The decision to emigrate from one's native country to a new land surely involves what economists call benefit-cost analysis. What do you think are the key factors for a potential migrant to consider (on both the benefit and cost sides) in this analysis? What information might someone making this decision need to make it correctly? Do you think people usually have access to this information? How might they get it?

5. Describe what is meant by the phrase "underground economy," and give a real-world example. Clearly, legal policy will affect whether a certain economic activity is conducted "underground" or "aboveground," but what economic forces need to be present as well? In the real-world example you identified, describe how the illegality of the activity affects the well-being of (a) illegal workers, (b) legal workers, (c) employers, and (d) consumers.

CHAPTER 4

Profits in the Political Marketplace

*Is Government Regulation the Secret
to Competitive Success?*

by Nicholas L. Centanni

All politics are based on the indifference of the majority.

—JAMES RESTON

Chapter Highlights

- Competitive Strategy
- Product Differentiation
- Public Choice Theory
- Antitrust
- Rent Seeking

I like you. Though we've never met, I'm sure you're intelligent, open-minded, and highly motivated. How do I know? You picked up this book, didn't you? So I'm going to let you in on a little secret: how to become filthy rich.

Two words: energy drinks. You doubt me? Take a look around. Every third person is drinking one, and the other two just finished one or are on their way to 7-11 to buy one as you read this. America runs on . . . caffeine and corn syrup.

So let's suppose you've gratefully accepted my advice and tooled up to make energy drinks and bank huge profits. What might you find?

Maybe the first thing you'll notice is the competition. Consumers have lots of alternative energy boosters to choose from. I don't know about you, but even plain old coffee or lower-octane sodas achieve the desired result for me—a temporary, caffeinated high. But, you argue, "My energy drink is much better than those old-school drinks. So I won't have a problem convincing people to switch to my new, cutting-edge product, which is both cheaper and more exciting than coffee, soda, or other rocket fuel."[1]

Fine. But once people buy your product instead of those old-school drinks and you start banking profits, your competition is not going to stand still. Your product and your market will become the target of lots of other people who want a piece of the action. So they will imitate you— *maybe even copy your recipe!*—and start selling energy drinks, too.

What's worse, they might somehow figure out how to produce their drinks at a lower cost than you do, so they can offer theirs for a lower price. Those weasels. (While it seemed fair when you were taking others' market share, these newcomers just seem greedy, don't they?) You might also realize that some of these new rivals are foreign conglomerates trying to muscle in on your turf. All of a sudden, your profits are shrinking.

But before you attempt to sue me for dispensing bad business advice, I've got another, far more important tip. Sometimes, the real secret to riches—and riches that will *last*—is not just building a better mousetrap or mixing a better energy drink. That's not even a secret—it's a cliché. The problem here is the inevitable imitators, competitors, and rivals. How do you keep them from doing to you what you did to those old-school drink companies? Here's the secret: Democracy is your friend. Yet, what Winston Churchill called "the worst form of government, except for all those other forms that have been tried,"[2] can help make your business more profitable, though maybe not necessarily in a virtuous way. In the next sections, I'll map out a path to profit that goes through government offices and show why it might be successful.

Shopping at the Political Marketplace

The first move in this game is a proverbial no-brainer. You need to keep those foreign conglomerates where they belong—someplace foreign—so you should dial up your representatives in Congress.

What can they do? If you've been watching the news in recent years, you know they can give you some money to stave off bankruptcy. But we don't want to be *too* bold—and, anyway, your company is not failing just yet, much less "too big to fail."[3] Since your immediate problem is the invasion of those foreign conglomerates, you need your lawmakers to place a tariff[4] on energy drinks coming from other countries to make sure

---

1 Jargon alert: You have "differentiated your product" from the competition, so while there are substitutes for your drink, they aren't *perfect* substitutes.

2 Winston Churchill in a speech to the House of Commons on November 11, 1947.

3 This was the criterion used to justify bailouts of some of the larger banks and two of the three U.S. automakers following the financial crisis of 2007–2008. The logic was that allowing these firms to go bankrupt would have caused so much macroeconomic pain—unemployment, investment portfolio losses, etc.—that taxpayer-financed subsidies were a good idea.

4 For some reason, a tax on imported goods is known as a tariff—probably to make it sound less objectionable.

that you—a patriotic, homegrown supplier—won't be undersold. As long as this import tax is set high enough, it'll make your energy drink cheaper than the foreign versions and protect your profits.

Of course, this will make consumers worse off. Aside from higher prices on imported drinks, they'll probably have fewer brands and flavors to choose from once this law goes into effect. So why would your elected representatives do your bidding and impose this tariff? Energy drinkers are many, as we have already noted, and you are just one of their constituents. Since democracy means the majority rules, won't all those consumers get mad at politicians who cause them harm and vote the rascals out of office? Won't your elected representatives realize this and tell you to forget about your import tax?

Relax. For reasons I'll describe in more detail later, there are no worries about that happening. And if the foreign conglomerates hire lobbyists to argue about all this, you've got a pretty good story to tell: Your company employs quite a few workers in your representatives' districts, and their jobs are at risk. Their votes are at risk, too. In sum, the foreign competition problem seems solvable with an appropriate policy obtained in the political marketplace.

But that still leaves your *domestic* competition problem. Is there anything that can be done about companies here in the good ole USA making similar energy drinks? Sure, you could do things the old-fashioned way. Maybe an ad blitz, with flashy commercials claiming your rivals are not up to your high standards of quality, could increase your sales. Or a PR campaign highlighting how the competition exploits their workers while you treat your "associates" like royalty and, as icing on the cake, donate large amounts to the political causes favored by people that your marketing research tells you is your "target demographic." Some of that might work, but, let's face it, it's been done to death lately.

I recommend a more reliable approach: Keep working with those lawmakers. There's a lot they can do to make your competitive life easier, most of it involving what economists call "erecting barriers to entry." For example, you could convince lawmakers to require new sellers of energy drinks to get a license certifying that they are meeting government standards (with, of course, a grandfather clause specifying that existing sellers, who have an established track record, are already licensed). Or you could ask them to tell industry regulators to write rules that make it more difficult and costly for imitators to poach market share.

If you are really bold, you might ask lawmakers to let you and your fellow energy drink makers to get together and "cooperate," setting certain industry standards that make it easier for you all to do business while, at the same time, harder from someone not currently on the inside to get a toehold in this market. If you did this without government help, a lot of this kind of thing might be illegal under federal antitrust laws, which prohibit business practices that limit entry into your market or otherwise harm consumers. But it's your constitutional right to ask the government to do these things—and if it agrees, it's all good (and legal).

Again, many of these entry barriers will have little or nothing to do with actually helping consumers—and some might harm them. So, again, the question is this: Would the government go along with your diabolical plans? And if so, why?

IGNORANCE IS ~~BLISS~~ RATIONAL (SOMETIMES)

Our day-to-day lives are often hectic and stressful. Whether we are holding down a full- or part-time job (and consider school a job with deferred compensation), there never seems to be enough time to work, take care of family and personal responsibilities, and keep up with priorities like following our favorite sports teams, tuning in to celebrity gossip, or constantly updating our Facebook pages. For most people, "keeping track of what my elected representatives are up to today" is an item that's pretty far down the to-do list—or maybe not even on it at all. In fact, some surveys have found that less than half of us even know who our chief representatives are.[5]

But I'm not going to judge people. It's perfectly understandable—even rational—for us *not* to pay much attention to politics (the term coined for this is "rational ignorance"). It takes time away from other activities, it's not fun (unless you are a political junkie, which I have to admit I am, sort of), and it gets you very little. If someone pays really close attention to all kinds of political issues and becomes a very well-informed voter, what good does that do? When was the last time an election swung the other way because of one vote? True, if everybody thought that way and decided to stop paying attention or voting, we would be in a mess, but we are not talking about everybody (yet). For individuals, the costs of learning all the ins and outs of a particular policy or candidate for office and then expressing our preferences by voting or writing letters to elected officials usually far exceed the benefits.[6]

THE IN CROWD

Our representatives not only know this, but they take advantage of it. The key force here—as reliable as gravity—is self-interest. There are exceptions to every generalization, but it's a good bet to assume that people

---

5 We're so apathetic about politics that in the historic and electrifying 2008 presidential election, just over 60 percent of the eligible voters bothered to go to the polls, according to a George Mason University study. Usually turnout is even lower than that—and when we do vote, our knowledge of the candidates who aren't at the top of the ballot is sketchy. See, for example, http://elections.gmu.edu/Turnout_2008G.html.

6 There's an entire field of economics devoted to studying why voters, politicians, and government officials act as they do, known as "public choice theory." James Buchanan won a Nobel Prize in 1986 for his role in developing the field, but others such as Duncan Black, Gordon Tullock, Kenneth Arrow, and Mancur Olson contributed greatly to its development.

know where their individual interests lie and, though they're sometimes wrong, act in ways that serve them. In the political marketplace, though, this can produce some very odd results.

As we've just seen, when individual voters act in self-interest, this can mean they don't even vote! When they do, they are usually motivated by an issue that's near and dear to their hearts—and they ignore lots of other stuff in which their representatives might get involved. Like energy drink regulation. As a result, officeholders can do a lot of things that fly under the radar—which they will, if it is in *their* self-interest to do so. Meanwhile, you are trying to protect your profits by thinking of ways to make your reps decide that voting for the tariffs or regulations you want will be good for them politically. That's not hard: You'll definitely write some campaign contribution checks if you decide they're worthy, you'll lobby your friends in other industries to do the same (and promise to return the favor when similar taxes or regulations benefiting them are on the agenda), and you'll encourage all your employees and their families to get with the program, writing sincere letters of support for the policies that will help protect their jobs.

The bottom line is that a very *large* number of eligible voters, even though they'll wind up paying higher prices (or facing more limited choices) when they buy their energy drinks, are likely to be outmaneuvered in the political marketplace by a much *smaller* number of people. Because there are so many consumers, the costs of the tariffs or regulations that will prop up your company's profits will be spread thin. Those consumers have decided, in effect, that they'd rather pay those costs than the even larger costs of (oh, noooo!) getting politically involved. On the other hand, the profits resulting from policies will be divided among a much smaller group—basically you, your employees, and your industry allies—that will have a much stronger incentive to lobby, vote, and get what it wants in the political marketplace. Pundits call this "special interest" groups; they're a political "in crowd" that often abuses the greater public interest.

So there's the secret: Use the government to rig the market in your favor. I'm not proud of recommending it—in fact, I'm hoping you don't actually use it as a business tactic. If you're going to get rich, I'd rather you did it in a way we could all be proud of.

Of course, you might be thinking that this whole scheme is a little unrealistic. I mean, a small minority taking advantage of the majority? In a majority-rules system? Seems unlikely that anything like this scenario happens in the real world.

Got Milk?

Milk is way more wholesome than energy drinks. We've been told all our lives that it builds strong bones and teeth, so it's good for you even if it doesn't help you stay awake on a long drive or when you're studying for a test. And those in the milk business are equally wholesome; they're farmers, people of the land, solid citizens. They'd never stoop to the kind of price-increasing, consumer-abusing tactics I described earlier, right?

Sure they would—and they do. In fact, they've devised new tactics and perfected them all. Dairy farmers have faced the competitive problems I described earlier in the energy drink market for over a century. One farmer would set up an operation on the outskirts of a town, bank nice profits by delivering fresh, nutritious milk to eager consumers, and then, attracted by those profits, someone else would buy some cows, supply more milk, and prices and profits would fall. Nice for those milk drinkers, but a major pain for the farmers. Eventually (way back in the 1930s), they took exactly the same path I mapped out for energy drink makers: Get the government involved.[7]

Unfortunately, "involved" doesn't begin to describe the work the government does for dairy farmers. The U.S. Department of Agriculture has divvied up the country into eleven regions, and every month it sets minimum prices for fluid milk and other dairy products in each one under its Federal Milk Marketing Order system. By law, then, no dairy farmer can steal market share from another by offering consumers a better deal. In other markets, this would be called price fixing, and its practitioners would be prosecuted by the U.S. Department of Justice or the Federal Trade Commission for violating antitrust laws. But, as I noted earlier, if you get the government to do this for you, you don't get into trouble. That doesn't mean it's good for society, though.[8]

But wait, there's more. If consumers decide dairy prices are too high and leave farmers' products on the shelves, there's no need to have a sale. Under its "Milk Price Support Program," the U.S.D.A. will step in and buy any unsold inventory of storable dairy products at the fixed price. Then there is also the Milk Income Loss Contract Program (MILC—get it?), which provides cash subsidies to dairy farmers if, somehow, those fixed prices aren't generating enough profit. Finally, there are tariffs that keep pesky foreign competitors from stealing market share and a Dairy Export Incentive Program that pays cash subsidies to U.S. dairy farmers who sell in foreign markets.

Sweet deal. Unless you're a milk drinker. One study by the Organisation for Economic Co-operation and Development (OECD) found that these programs amount to a 26 percent implicit tax on dairy consumers.

---

7 Blaney, Don P., and Manchester, Alden C. "Milk Pricing in the United States." USDA Economic Research Service. *Agriculture Information Bulletin*, no. AIB761 (February 2001). Available at www.ers.usda.gov/publications/aib761/aib761c.pdf; Edwards, Chris. "Milk Madness." Cato Institute. *Tax & Budget Bulletin*, no. 47 (July 2007). Available at www.cato.org/pubs/tbb/tbb_0707_47.pdf.

8 For example, we correctly call OPEC (Organization of Petroleum Exporting Countries) a cartel, and when its members get together to fix minimum prices for oil, we're indignant because we know this will harm consumers. Dairy farmers obviously have a better PR firm, though.

And a regressive tax, at that, since low-income families spend proportionately more of their income on dairy and other food products and so pay a greater relative burden. A Government Accountability Office (GAO) study concluded that U.S. consumers typically pay 30 percent more for nonfat dry milk, 50 percent more for cheese, and 100 percent more for butter than world market averages.[9]

When I rant about this to friends, their usual response is that if we don't prop up dairy prices this way, "we'll have no milk." Wrong. Oh, it's true that without all this protection from competition and without the price and income supports dairy farmers have bought in the political marketplace *some* might go out of business—but just the least efficient, highest-cost ones. The rest of the world is not doomed to a butterless, cheeseless, and milkless existence because their prices are lower; they just get their supplies from the most efficient producers.

Another friend of mine worries about my lack of sympathy for the little guy. "Hey, why pick on the small farmers?" she asks. "They work hard and don't make very much." Except there's one problem: Most farmers today are not "little guys." It's true that about 98 percent of all farms in the United States are classified as "family farms,"[10] but the image this brings to most minds differs from the reality. According to a 2009 USDA report, "ten percent of family farms that grossed at least $250,000 accounted for 80 percent of the value of production."[11] So most of our food comes from sizeable operations that are making good money. The same study found that 'in 2009, average family farm household income was $77,169"— which was nearly 55 percent higher than the median U.S. household income that year."'

In sum, agricultural policies like those I've described for the dairy industry raise prices to large numbers of people who are, on average, less well off than the small number of people who benefit. And we let it happen.

SOME BETTER ADVICE

While it's true that we live in a system where the majority rules, the majority that's *relevant* is made up of people who (a) pay attention and (b) bother to be politically active. They might be few in number, but they are high in influence. There are, for example, just about 2 million farmers in this country and over 300 million eaters.[12] But because those eaters

9 OECD. "Agricultural Policies in OECD Countries: Monitoring and Evaluation, 2005," p. 294; GAO. "Dairy Industry: Information on Milk Prices, Factors Affecting Prices, and Dairy Policy Options." GAO-05-50 (December 29, 2004), p. 106.
10 Economic Research Service/USDA. "Structure and Finances of U.S. Farms: 2005 Family Farm Report." Available at www.ers.usda.gov/publications/EIB12/EIB12c.pdf?
11 USDA. "Farm Household Economics and Well-Being: Farm Household Income." Available at www.ers.usda.gov/Briefing/WellBeing/farmhouseincome.htm#typology.
12 USDA. "Census of Agriculture Shows Growing Diversity in U.S. Farming." Release no. 0036.09. Available at www.usda.gov/wps/portal/!ut/p/_s.7_0_A/7_0_1OB?conten tid=2009/02/0036.xml&contentidonly=true.

think the costs of transacting in the political marketplace (and keeping the government from enacting policies that pump up their food prices) are greater than the benefits, a small minority becomes the majority, dictates public policy, and determines how an enormous amount of the country's income and resources are allocated.

Unfortunately, it's not just farmers who have figured out how to use the government to acquire greater profits.[13] You name the industry—energy, health care, transportation, insurance, finance, communication—and it has a major presence in Washington, DC, these days. *They* pay close attention to politics and policy, and our elected representatives pay close attention to them.

So . . . what about us? Is there any way to level the playing field a bit? Well, you'll be glad to know that the people who analyze the political marketplace for a living are hard at work trying to do exactly that, with a field they call constitutional economics. Among other things, they're thinking of rules that might enhance voters' incentives to be informed and get involved and that might reduce the frequency of policies that benefit an "in crowd" at voters' expense. If more policy decisions are made at the local or state level rather than nationally, for example, voters might see that they have a greater stake in these decisions and pay more attention to the debates surrounding them.

But if the political marketplace is going to function more efficiently, we're just going to have to do a better job as consumers, voters, and business decision makers. Thanks to the Internet, of course, learning about the issues and the policies that affect us is cheaper than ever. It can even be fun. As I said before, I'm kind of a political junkie; I actually enjoy getting together with people—those I agree with politically, and those I don't—to discuss all kinds of issues. And online, the discussions can get regional, national, and even global. So I'd say technology is helping us deal with the "rational ignorance" problem at the individual level—but we can certainly do more in this regard.

What would also help is more ethical behavior from our business leaders. Instead of pleading for insulation from competition, they should relish it. There are lots of entrepreneurs out there looking for ways to make life better for everyone by rolling out the latest and greatest "big new thing." For every person who comes up with something hugely successful, a hundred might fail. But if someone tries to compete with that new product or service, it should be welcomed by those already established and worn as badge of honor. Not only is "imitation the sincerest form of flattery,"[14] but it's also an incentive to do things better, be more creative, and do things that set you apart from crowd.

---

13 The scholars of public choice theory call this "rent-seeking behavior," since "economic rents" are payments for goods or factors of production in excess of their opportunity costs.

14 Colton, Charles Caleb. *Lacon: or Many Things in Few Words, Addressed to Those Who Think* (18th ed.). London: Longman, 1823.

For some examples, let's look back at the two beverages I talked about earlier in this chapter. C. J. Rapp originated high-caffeine Jolt cola back in 1985, while he was a student at SUNY Potsdam. Since that time, energy drinks have grown from a niche industry to one that banked $12.5 billion in revenue in 2010.[15] It's also interesting to note that major soft-drink manufacturers realized the potential of the energy drink market and responded by introducing new brands and innovating with new flavors to meet people's diverse tastes. Essentially, they were both imitating and improving on Rapp's product, and today the industry is growing at an impressive 33 percent a year![16]

The milk industry, on the other hand, with its "in-crowd" of complacent dairy farmers and protective government regulators, has been doing things the same old way for decades—and, unsurprisingly, has seen annual per-capita consumption of its products drop from 45 gallons in 1945 to about half that today.[17]

In the long run, then, using the political marketplace to secure your market position carries no guarantees of success. Staying competitive and innovative might be a better bet.

READ ON/JOIN UP

➤ There is a good amount of information about companies using government to secure profits in this book:

Rivoli, Pietra. *The Travels of a T-shirt in the Global Economy: An Economist Examines the Markets, Power and Politics of World Trade.* Hoboken, NJ: John Wiley & Sons, 2005.

➤ One of the foundations of modern public choice theory, this work looks at the similarities between the political marketplace and the marketplace of goods:

Downs, Anthony. *An Economic Theory of Democracy.* New York: Harper & Brothers, 1957.

➤ Another foundation of the public choice theory:

Tullock, Gordon. "The Welfare Costs of Tariffs, Monopolies, and Theft." *Western Economic Journal*, 1967, vol. 5, no. 3, pp. 224–232.

➤ A detailed account of almost every major antitrust case in the late 19th and 20th centuries, this book also provides examples of how corporations have used regulations against competitors in their respective industries:

Armentano, Dominick T. *Antitrust and Monopoly.* Oakland, CA: Independent Institute, 1999.

---

15 Cooke, George R. "Jolt: America's Original Energy Drink." University of Rochester, William Simon Graduate School of Business Administration Case Study, July 2009, p. 5.

16 Ibid.

17 Putnam, Judy, and Allshouse, Jane. "Trends in U.S. per Capita Consumption of Dairy Products, 1909 to 2001." *Amber Waves* (June 2003). Available at www.ers.usda.gov/AmberWaves/June03/DataFeature/.

➢ This book provides a reader with an understanding of not just "rent seekers" in the political marketplace but many other economic foundations:

Hazlitt, Henry. *Economics in One Lesson*. New York: Harper & Brothers, 1946.

A writer for the New York Times, Henry Hazlitt was able to connect with the average reader.

➢ Another book to check out:

Brennan, Geoffrey, and Buchanan, James M. *The Reason of Rules: Constitutional Political Economy*. Indianapolis, IN: Liberty Fund, Inc., 2000.

QUESTIONS FOR DISCUSSION

1. The energy drink example at the beginning of the chapter suggests that market competition can be pretty rough, with many forces present that make it hard to earn a profit in the long run. Briefly review these forces, and then consider what ways you can defeat them (*apart* from relying on protection from competition that you might obtain in the political marketplace) and ensure that your energy drink company will earn persistently high profits for a long time.

2. Do you agree with economists that it can be "rational" to be ignorant about public policy or not to pay close attention to political affairs? What will be the long-run consequences of such behavior, even if "rational"?

3. If it is true that public policies are exchanged in a "political marketplace," who are the demanders and suppliers of these policies? Give specific examples. In what ways is behavior in this marketplace similar to or different from that in more ordinary, economic markets? Are there some characteristics of (or incentives in) the political marketplace that invite people to behave differently in this setting?

4. Voter participation rates in U.S. elections are often below 50 percent. Some countries *require* their citizens to vote in order to address the problem of low participation or "rational abstention." Do you think this would, in the United States, improve how the political marketplace functions? Why or why not?

5. Suppose it is true that U.S. cheese prices are 50 percent above the world average, per the GAO study cited in footnote 9. This suggests that some U.S. cheese makers bank higher profits than they would without USDA help—that is, they earn "economic rents." How would these cheese makers respond to proposals to eliminate the USDA's milk programs? How much would they spend to preserve their "rents"? Will this sort of behavior alter the judgment about whether it is a good idea to change USDA's milk policies?

CHAPTER 5

The $1,200 Sticks

Supply, Demand, and the Economics
of Prohibition

by Crystal A. Callahan

*The struggle for public security is a battle that will take time,
money, and also, regrettably, human lives.*

—FELIPE CALDERON,
PRESIDENT OF MEXICO[1]

Chapter Highlights

- Externalities
- Laws of Supply and Demand
- Price Elasticity of Demand and Expenditure
- Rational Choice
- The Law of Unintended Consequences

One afternoon I walked into my dorm room to find my roommate's boyfriend crying.

Oh, no, I thought, *she dumped him.* Since I'm not a relationship expert, my first impulse was to pretend not to notice. Fairly quickly, though, guilt—and perhaps curiosity—took over, and I decided to ask him what was wrong.

"Hey, what's up?" I asked cautiously.

"I just lost twelve hundred dollars," he blubbered.

Whew. No breakup consolation necessary. "How'd you do that?" I inquired.

"I can't believe it. You're going to think I'm really stupid. And it wasn't even all my money—I collected it from friends around the dorm."

"I'll try not to judge you," I promised, wondering how hard that would be.

---

1 Taber, Jane. *Ottawa Notebook.* May 27, 2010. Available at www.theglobeandmail.com/news/
politics/ottawa-notebook/mexican-president-vows-to-help-resolve-visa-feud/article1582835/.

"Well, I was trying to buy weed for my friends. This guy on the street, um, he tricked me and didn't give me the right stuff."

"What do you mean he didn't give you the right stuff?" I responded. "Were you supposed to get really fancy pot or something?"

"Um . . . see, he actually didn't give me the weed at all. He gave me a paper bag full of little sticks."

Wow—$1,200 for sticks. Probably a world record. At first I considered this guy's story totally ridiculous. What type of person loses that kind of money?[2] I even felt a little envious of the dealer. Why should *that* guy make $1,200 for 2 minutes of stick-gathering when it takes me three weeks to make that much working at the mall (before taxes!)?

But then I started to analyze the situation. There's no question that drugs are bad. We ban them for that very reason. Banning them, however, doesn't make them disappear, and there are many unintended side effects of our prohibition strategy. The big question is whether these side effects can be so significant that we should reassess whether the ban is worthwhile—or, at least, worthwhile in its present form. This chapter provides some guidance for how to think about prohibition by looking at supply-and-demand factors, the elasticity of demand, tradeoffs and externalities, and finally at the ban's unintended consequences.

IT'S GOOD TO BE A GANGSTA[3]

In an ideal world, making something illegal would cause sellers to stop supplying it and consumers to stop demanding it—completely. Problem solved. In the real world, though, the laws of supply and demand do not work exactly as we might like them to. For example, when law enforcement authorities succeed in reducing the amount of illegal drugs available, the drugs' prices go up. These increases can make selling them more profitable, attract more sellers, and make enforcement of the prohibition more difficult. On the buyers' side, higher prices might mean less quantity will be demanded, but since we're talking about addictive substances, even huge price increases won't completely deter some buyers. The illicit nature of a drug might also be a selling point; people may be attracted to it simply because they're not allowed to have it. Supply and demand can be complicated, especially when you're dealing with illegal substances.

---

2 The kind that gets mocked in sitcoms: Remember *The Office* (season five, episode eight, if you want to Hulu it) when Michael tries to frame Toby by planting a baggie of pot in his desk? A few clever delivery men trick Michael into purchasing $500 worth of "weed" that upon further inspection turns out to be caprice salad.

3 Well, maybe it feels good in theory, but in reality, small-time drug peddlers don't often make much of a life for themselves in the business. It's really the bosses that make out well, while the smaller guys make meager salaries. See the chapter entitled Why Do Drug Dealers Still Live with Their Moms? in Levitt, Steven, and Dubner, Stephen J., *Freakonomics: A Rogue Economist Explores the Hidden Side of Everything*. New York: William Morrow/HarperCollins, 2005.

Luckily, economists have tools that can help us sort things out. One of the most important, known as the "price elasticity of demand," relates changes in quantity demanded to changes in an item's price.[4] You can measure the relationship for a particular good using historical data, and then use the relationship to predict the effects of future price changes. If people don't reduce their purchases of a good very much when its price goes up, we say demand is *inelastic*. Demand is *elastic* if people buy a lot less as a good's price increases. For example, the elasticity of demand for gasoline has been calculated as –0.26 (which is highly inelastic), so if gas prices go up 10 percent we buy just 2.6 percent less gas.[5] That's often the way it is when there aren't many good substitutes for a product.

Since the goal of drug prohibition is to reduce the amount consumed, it would be nice if demand were very elastic. If the price of drugs increased, perhaps by preventing some amount from being produced or transported or by making it more costly to do so, then there would be large reductions in the amount demanded.

Naturally, given the illegality of drug sales, there's limited historical data available to precisely estimate elasticity. But, unfortunately, the news we do have is not good: The best estimates are that the demand for drugs is highly *in*elastic.[6] When we're handing out blame for the bad side effects of illegal drug markets, we should not overlook demanders. They're not only willing to break the law, but they are not much discouraged by higher prices.

Because of the inelastic nature of drug demand, dealers can still make money when drug enforcement reduces supply. If the police intercept, say, 10 percent of dealers' products before they reach potential customers, you'd think that would hurt the bottom line.[7] To the contrary, because drug demand is so price inelastic, it's likely that prices would rise by more than 10 percent. The revenue gain from these higher prices would

---

4 Technically, it's a ratio: the percent change in quantity demanded divided by the percent change in price. Because consumers buy less when a product's price increases (and vice versa), the price elasticity of demand for that product will always be a negative number.

5 Espey, Molly. "Explaining the Variation in Elasticity Estimates of Gasoline Demand in the United States: A Meta-analysis." *Energy Journal*, 1996, vol. 17, no. 3, pp. 49–60. This is an estimate of our sensitivity to gas price changes in the short run; over time, as we figure out more ways to economize on gas usage (e.g., get a smaller car, move closer to work or school), our elasticity of demand tends to be greater. The long-run elasticity of demand for gas is –0.58, so a 10 percent price increase would cause us to reduce our gas consumption by 5.8 percent—more than twice as much as we would in the short run.

6 For example, estimates of the price elasticity of demand for marijuana among high school seniors range from –0.3 to –0.7. This means that if we raised price by 10 percent, kids in high school would only buy 3 to 7 percent less marijuana. See: Grossman, Michael, Chaloupka, Frank J., and Shim, Kyumin. "Illegal Drug Use And Public Policy," *Health Affairs*, vol. 21, no. 2 (March 2002), pp. 134–145.

7 And it might—if you're the unlucky dealer whose stock is confiscated in a bust, or if evading busts pushes your costs up faster than prices.

offset the losses (if any) from lower quantity sold.[8] That's a very unfortunate side effect. We're limiting the supply of drugs that make it to market, thus raising prices and increasing the amount of revenue flowing to dealers. As a result, the dealers have more cash to reinvest in their businesses. Maybe they'll spend the extra money on things like guns, which will come in handy if rival sellers try to move into their territories.

In legal markets, businesses compete by (generally) wholesome means, such as lower prices, better quality, attention-getting billboards, TV ads, or attractive storefronts. But drug dealers can't increase their market share by putting up signs or buying commercial time. How do they drive out the competition and increase sales and profits with more than just a "word of mouth" campaign? Unfortunately, many turn to physical violence. If you're already doing something illegal, it probably seems like a logical step.

So we face a dilemma—or, in economic parlance, a tradeoff. The whole point of making drugs illegal is to save lives. We don't want Joe College (or perhaps even Joe High School) to ruin his life with a drug habit. We *want* it to be hard and/or expensive to get things like marijuana, cocaine, heroin. You might say, therefore, that prohibition is doing what it is supposed to do: making drugs more expensive and less accessible. That's just part of the story, however. Some of the incentives we've inadvertently built into these illegal markets lead to some grave costs, including lives lost, that we can't ignore.

TRADEOFFS AND SPILLOVERS

Before we get too far into a discussion of the tangible costs and benefits of drug prohibition, though, I should mention some *in*tangibles—like freedom. Let me start with a caveat: I don't condone drug use. I'm not recommending you come home from class or work every day and light up a joint; I wouldn't use drugs even if they were legal. Drugs wreck many lives. Most of us get that.

Yet no matter how many Drug Abuse Resistance Education (DARE) programs we run in schools, or how many antidrug ads we run on television and in newspapers and magazines, we still haven't eradicated the demand for drugs. Maybe, when it comes to the desire to "get high," some people are incapable of making rational choices. They take unnecessary risks, and many become addicted and lose their jobs, abandon their families, and waste all their savings on their habit. Not good for them and not good for society.

When we make personal decisions, most of us are pretty good at figuring out what the results of our actions might be. We know we risk extra

---

8 Do the math: If the price elasticity of demand is –0.5 (the midpoint of the estimates discussed in footnote 5, above), then prices have to rise by 20 percent to reduce quantity demand by 10 percent. And since revenue is price times quantity sold, if you sell 10 percent less quantity at prices that are 20 percent higher, your revenue goes up.

poundage or higher cholesterol when we eat a cheeseburger and can usually decide whether those side effects are worth the greasy indulgence. But with respect to drugs, we're apparently not very good at making the right decision—at least some of us. When a great many members of society can't seem to resist something bad, we usually look to the government to keep it away. I've spoken with fellow students about the need for the "war on drugs," and just about all are confident that prohibition is appropriate. One friend's comment sums it up: "It's just wrong to legalize something that's so bad for people."

But when we make decisions for other people, even if it's to protect them from their own bad choices, we're limiting their freedom. When and how should we decide to trust the government to make decisions for us? Current drug policy reflects the belief that limiting our freedom of choice here is a good thing; no doubt it protects many people from self-inflicted harm. Some people, however, are hesitant to let the government intervene in any part of their lives, be it the chemicals they put in their bodies, whether they must wear a seatbelt while driving, or when they're allowed to have their first drink. To them, the principle is the same in each case: There are risks and rewards, costs and benefits, and they're reluctant to give up their freedom to choose. Where should we draw the line? I don't have the answer, but our decision shouldn't ignore the fact that it involves a tradeoff and that some people might regard the loss of their right to make even a bad decision (like using drugs) a steep cost.

Those who argue that prohibition is the right thing to do point out that there are *two* key benefits: It not only protects some potential users from themselves, but it also protects other people from users. They understand that the effects of drugs are not confined to those foolish enough to use them. They fear "spillover costs"—what economists call "negative externalities" —from others' decisions to use drugs.

An externality is basically a spillover effect that our actions have on someone else. For example, if I play loud music in my dorm room, my neighbors will hear it through the paper-thin walls. Assuming that my taste in music does not match their preferences, *they* will be annoyed and pay a cost for *my* actions. In much more serious ways, drug users can impose costs on innocent bystanders[9] such as their friends, family, employers, and neighbors when they drive impaired, fall behind at school or in the workplace, or resort to crime to finance their habits.

Unfortunately, as I suggested at the end of the previous section, the fact is that there are spillover costs from prohibition just as there are from the individual drug user's behavior. These costs can be very tangible, and very high. In trying to limit the damage of drug use, we have to consider both the nature and amount of these other, perhaps less obvious, "external costs."

---

9 These bystanders are "external" to the actions undertaken by, in this case, drug users. That explains economists' somewhat obscure terminology here—this is an "externality problem."

THE REAL FAIRY TALE

We don't have to look very hard to see the downsides of the drug war. The government spends over $30 billion annually to enforce the prohibition of drugs.[10] Fighting the drug war consumes an enormous amount of law enforcement resources, from police officers to prison space to lawyers and court time—all of which have valuable alternative uses. According to FBI data, there were more than 1.6 million arrests for drug abuse violations in 2009.[11] What would happen if all these resources were reassigned to fighting other kinds of crime? Would our streets be safer?

Many people might say no. We tend to think that the war on drugs keeps the lid on violent crime and that we need to spend even more on drug law enforcement to reduce homicide rates. Perhaps surprisingly, the evidence points to the contrary. Violent crime rates and drug law enforcement efforts seem to be *positively* correlated: When the drug war escalates, so does the homicide rate.[12]

This is an example of the law of unintended consequences. Quite often, when we take action to solve one problem, we accidentally cause another. Like when we take a couple of aspirin to treat a headache, sometimes we get an upset stomach as a result. When we're dealing with complicated things like public policies and their interactions with unpredictable human beings, such effects can be understandably hard to foresee.

With respect to illegal drugs, economists have found that enforcement efforts can "upset the equilibrium" in local markets. Taking down one drug dealer seems to invite violent competition for his turf among rivals; again, these "firms" can't compete for the newly available market through legal means, so they use illegal ones. As a result, Harvard economist Jeffrey Miron estimates that legalizing drugs might actually cut the homicide rate in the United States by 25 to 75 percent.[13]

Unfortunately, the spillover costs of drug prohibition are being paid beyond our borders, as well. Mexican president Felipe Calderon summarized the consequences of the drug war in his country rather well in the quotation at the start of the chapter: increased crime, political corruption, wealth transfers to drug lords, and diminished health standards. As the Mexican government has increased enforcement of prohibition by going on the offensive against large drug cartels in recent years, violence in the country has surged. Drug-related crime led to more than 5,300 deaths in

---

10 Miron, Jeffrey A. *Drug War Crimes: The Consequences of Prohibition*. Oakland, CA: The Independent Institute, 2004, p. 11.

11 Federal Bureau of Investigation. *Crime in the United States*. Available at www2.fbi.gov/ucr/cius2009/arrests/index.html.

12 Miron, p. 11.

13 Miron, p. 51. Let's take the midpoint of that range—a 50 percent reduction. Since there were over 15,000 murders in the United States in 2009, we're talking about saving 7,500 lives annually if Miron's analysis is valid.

Mexico in 2008, 7,600 in 2009, and about 12,500 by November of 2010. In total, there have been more than 30,100 casualties in the drug war since President Calderon took office in December 2006.[14]

In one particularly gruesome episode, cartel gangsters beheaded 12 Mexican soldiers as retribution for the death of three of its gunmen. A bag containing the severed heads was found dumped at a shopping center, accompanied by a note that read, "For every one of mine you kill, I'm going to kill ten of yours."[15] Naturally, this spike in violence has led many to question the escalation of the drug war, and as a concession to public opinion Mexico decriminalized personal amounts of certain drugs such as marijuana, cocaine, and heroin in 2009.

THE MORE THINGS CHANGE...

We have struggled with this issue—and these tradeoffs—before, with a war on alcohol. In 1919, the 18th Amendment to the Constitution banned the sale, manufacture, transportation, and importation of alcoholic beverages in the United States. But less than 15 years later, the 21st Amendment ended the "Prohibition era." Why did the experiment end so quickly? The motive for the 18th Amendment was the same as for our current drug war: We wanted to save people from themselves, from addiction to a destructive substance. In fairly short order, however, it became clear that the resulting gain did not justify the unintended consequences.

The best estimates are that alcohol use declined modestly during Prohibition, by 10 to 20 percent. As with drugs today, enforcement efforts didn't eliminate alcohol demand but diverted it to organizations run by people willing to break the law. Similar to modern drug gangs, those organizations felt free to use violence as a competitive tactic.[16] As a result, there have been two significant spikes in homicide rates in U.S. history—during Prohibition in the 1920s and early 1930s and during the drug war of recent decades. Homicide rates fell after the repeal of the 18th Amendment in

---

14 Mexico's attorney general described the unintended consequences of his country's campaign against the drug cartels: "Such operations have succeeded in eliminating several very dangerous people and disrupting their organizations, however, they have also served to further upset the balance of power among Mexico's criminal organizations. This imbalance has increased the volatility of the country's security environment by creating a sort of vicious feeding frenzy among the various organizations as they seek to preserve their own turf or seize territory from rival organizations." *CNN.* "Mexican Drug War Deaths Surpass 30,100." December 17, 2010. Available at http://articles.cnn.com/2010-12-17/world/mexico.violence_1_drug-war-border-city-drug-related-violence?_s=PM:WORLD. Excerpt from "Mexico and the Cartel Wars in 2010" by Scott Stewart from the Stratfor website, December 16, 2010. Copyright © 2010 by Stratfor Global Intelligence. Reprinted with permission.

15 Ellingwood, Ken. "Mexico's Drug War: Remains of 12 Decapitated Men Found in Mexico." *Los Angeles Times,* December 22, 2008. Available at www.latimes.com/news/nationworld/world/la-fg-mexico-behead22-2008dec22,0,6725030.story.

16 For an entertaining example, HBO's fictional television show *Boardwalk Empire* dramatizes the Prohibition era.

1933—and increased dramatically beginning around 1970, a time of escalation in the drug war.[17]

It's also important to note that the end of Prohibition didn't mean the end of efforts to cope with the problems of alcohol abuse. We simply conceded that the alcohol market couldn't be eradicated and instead regulated it closely and taxed it aggressively. Taxes raised prices and reduced quantity demanded compared to pre-Prohibition levels—and diverted revenue away from bootleggers into government coffers. Today, no one is petitioning the White House with grandiose proposals to bring back the 18th Amendment and rid the country of alcohol.

What's so different about drugs? Whether you live in a city, suburbia, or rural America, there's evidence of the "spillover costs" of drug prohibition in virtually every daily newspaper or on the nightly news. As much publicity as there is about the terrible things that happen when people do drugs, there's also plenty of news about the collateral damage in the drug war. So why are we so reluctant to deescalate this war in the same way we did with alcohol back in 1933?

Maybe we're just afraid of the unknown—and it's clear that there are a lot of unanswered questions about drug policy. If drugs were legalized, how much would prices fall? How much would consumption rise? Demand may be inelastic now—and, so, increases in quantity demand might be smaller, proportionately, than any price decreases—but that might not hold up if prices change dramatically.[18] So we don't know for sure whether heavy taxation can even replace prohibition as a discourager of demand, much less whether it can make drugs more scarce and expensive than they are now.

You can probably think of dozens more practical questions that would have to be answered if we seriously considered major changes to our drug policy. The good news, though, is that the tools of economics and cost-benefit analysis can answer a lot of those questions. It's time to get busy using those tools.

READ ON/JOIN UP

➤ A concise and easy-to-read overview of Prohibition, including its effects and suggested next steps, can be found here:

Miron, Jeffrey A. *Drug War Crimes: The Consequences of Prohibition*. Oakland, CA: The Independent Institute, 2004.

➤ For an entertaining and thought-provoking look into the hierarchy of drug gangs, see:

---

17 See Miron, Jeffrey A. "Violence and the U.S. Prohibitions of Drugs and Alcohol." *American Law and Economics Review*, vol. 1 (Fall 1999), pp. 78–114.

18 In addition, the illegality of drugs might be limiting demand: In economics jargon, if it became less risky to experiment with drugs, the whole demand curve might shift outward, no matter how "price inelastic" the current demand curve is.

Levitt, Steven, and Dubner, Stephen J. *Freakonomics: A Rogue Economist Explores the Hidden Side of Everything.* New York: William Morrow/HarperCollins, 2005.

➤ For quick links to the Web sites discussed below, please visit *www.pearsonhighered.com/walters*:

Another concise overview of Prohibition, focusing on its effects and potential repeal, is available to read in its full form on Mises. See Thornton, Mark. *The Economics of Prohibition.* University of Utah Press, 1991.

A great study on Portugal's experiment with the decriminalization of drugs is available from the CATO Institute.

An interesting parallel is drawn between the drug war and the cigarette industry at the *New York Times.*

A look at unintended consequences in Texas border towns can be found in the *Wall Street Journal.*

For all the avid bloggers out there, check out Projects on LA Times, Crawford on Drugs, and Border Violence Analysis.

QUESTIONS FOR DISCUSSION

1. My roommate's boyfriend experienced one of the unintended consequences of drug prohibition: "adulterated quality" of the product that is exchanged illegally. Could this transaction have gone even worse for him? In legal markets for potentially harmful products (like cigarettes or alcohol), is this sort of problem present to the same extent? Why or why not?

2. Brainstorm an alternative to total drug prohibition in the United States. What potential pros and cons (i.e., what tradeoffs) are there in your plan?

3. Some of the research cited in the chapter concludes that the price elasticity of demand for drugs is low (i.e., demand is inelastic). With this in mind, draw a sketch of a "drug demand curve," with quantity demanded on the horizontal axis and price on the vertical axis, and show how a price increase or decrease will affect the total amount spent on drugs (and received by drug sellers). As drug prices rise or fall, will the price elasticity of demand necessarily stay the same?

4. Identify as many of the external costs of the sale and consumption of illegal drugs as you can. Would any of these external costs be reduced or eliminated if drugs could be exchanged legally? Why or why not?

5. Research the drug policy in three other countries of your choice. Evaluate the policy's effectiveness, considering data on (a) violent and nonviolent crime, (b) incarceration rates, (c) drug prices, and (d) drug consumption.

CHAPTER 6

All You Can Eat

Demand and Supply at the Healthcare Buffet

by John J. Walters

In a country as wealthy as ours, for us to have people who are going bankrupt because they can't pay their medical bills . . . there's something fundamentally wrong about that.

—PRESIDENT BARACK OBAMA,
SPEAKING DURING THE 2008 PRESIDENTIAL DEBATE

Chapter Highlights

- Marginal Benefits and Costs
- Health Economics
- Moral Hazard
- Adverse Selection
- The Samaritan's Dilemma

"Look," my friend would say, "it's the regulars." He'd nod his head toward the entrance of the Great Fortune Chinese Buffet as a few particularly rotund customers lumbered in. It was a line I heard every time we ate there, but the plain fact was that we were regulars, too. Seven bucks and all the orange chicken and shrimp lo mein you can eat? That was enough for me—though, after a couple years of steadily declining quality and regular roach sightings, I haven't bellied up to the buffet in a while.

Not that I don't think about that rude but apt line every time I see a Golden Corral commercial or find myself in a restaurant that offers all-you-can-eat seafood on weekends. Ah, the sweet prospect of the "binge." I know that's why we were regulars. And, with the exception of a few folks with the willpower to sample just a little of everything, that's probably what got most everyone else in the door, too. It seems like such an irresistible deal. Until the almost inevitable stomachache that night. Or until weeks later, when we would work up the courage to step on a scale.

It might just be human nature to make these short-sighted decisions. We don't think of the long-run consequences as we go back for one more soda refill or one more serving of dessert. Why? Probably because it's more fun not to. Sometimes, though, the "system" actually encourages us to make those silly choices. In this case, since we all pay the same flat rate just to get inside, every extra plateful seems *free*, so we feel almost foolish if we don't eat until we really aren't enjoying the food much anymore. In economic terms, we eat until the value of another bite falls to match its price—zero.[1]

Meanwhile, the buffet owners face the challenge of figuring out ways to provide enough of what people want to eat while still turning a profit. On the surface, this doesn't seem too complicated. A buffet that finds the right balance between price and quality will thrive, while a buffet with bad food and high prices will go out of business. But what if the high-priced buffet is the only one in town? More important, what if the buffet is not for something we like but may not really need, like Chinese food, but something crucial, like heart surgery? Would that change our behavior as consumers? Let's find out.

The Systems of Our Neighbors

The healthcare systems in most developed countries look similar. Most people would be hard-pressed to tell the difference between your average Canadian, American, and European doctors or hospitals. The devil is in the details, however. Countries vary wildly regarding who pays for healthcare costs (government agencies or private companies) and the manner in which that care is administered.

Let's start by comparing our system in the United States, which relies on people to purchase private health insurance on their own, with that in Canada. As documentary filmmaker Michael Moore so elegantly demonstrated in his 2007 film, *SiCKO*, our system has some very visible and tragic shortcomings regarding affordability and access to care.

His solution: to "borrow the system of our neighbors" so that we no longer have anyone "slipping through the cracks." In effect, he wants to open a healthcare buffet, with one price (paid out of your—or, better still, someone else's—tax dollars) to get you in the door, and all the "free" medical attention you want after that, like they have in Canada.

In Moore's portrayal, Canadians are so afraid of the American healthcare system that they won't even hop across the border for lunch without purchasing short-term insurance. *Wow*, I thought as I watched his movie for the first time, *their system must be really great for them to fear losing it*

---

1 To make good decisions, we need to compare marginal benefits and marginal costs. Think of *marginal* benefits as the extra satisfaction you get from doing something a bit more. When we eat another bite of food, extend our vacation, or read the next chapter of a book, we're getting some extra benefit. But we're also paying an extra (*marginal*) cost, whether in money, time, or something else (like a stomachache). When the marginal cost of an action outweighs the marginal benefit, we tend to cut the activity out. Unless, perhaps, we get a misleading signal about costs—like at a buffet.

so badly. Either that, or ours must be really bad. I wondered which I would prefer and what makes our systems so different.

A major contrast is the length of the line at the buffet table. The Fraser Institute, an independent Canadian research and education organization, has surveyed patient wait times in Canada for 20 years and reported in 2010 that there was "a total waiting time of 18.2 weeks between referral from a general practitioner and elective treatment," which is "nearly 3 weeks longer than what [surveyed] physicians believe is 'reasonable' for elective treatment after an appointment with a specialist."[2] Where you live and what kind of care you need also matter a great deal. Overall wait times averaged only 14 weeks in Ontario but were 44.4 weeks in Prince Edward Island. And on average, patients would wait around 10 weeks for cardiovascular surgery but 35.6 weeks (almost 9 months!) for orthopedic surgery.

Unfortunately, the problem has been getting worse, with average wait times increasing 96 percent between 1993 and 2010. So, as you might expect, the Canadian government has been trying to make things more efficient, allocating $4.5 billion in taxpayer money to a Wait Times Reduction Fund in 2004.[3] So far, though, these expenditures haven't generated much improvement: in 2004, the average wait between an appointment with a specialist and treatment was 9.5 weeks, but in 2010 the wait had only dropped to 9.3 weeks. As a result, the surveyed specialists reported that 1 percent of their patients left Canada for treatment in other countries—most of them, it might surprise Mr. Moore to learn, went to the United States.[4]

We're not perfect, of course, but we do deliver care faster. One study found that 57 percent of Canadians wait more than 4 weeks to see a specialist, versus only 23 percent of Americans, and in Canada 42 percent of emergency room visits involve waits longer than 2 hours, versus 29 percent in the United States.[5] On average, Americans wait a mere 20.5 days to see medical specialists—and the ones who wait longest are those using government-provided Medicaid.[6]

Unfortunately, some waiting seems inevitable. Healthcare is, after all, a scarce good; our wants or needs for care may be almost infinite, but supply is limited.[7] Scarcity is generally dealt with in two ways. You can

---

2 Barua, Bacchus, Rovere, Mark, and Skinner, Brett J. "Waiting Your Turn: Wait Times for Health Care in Canada, 2010 Report." The Fraser Institute. December 2010, pp. 5–9.

3 Health Canada. "Wait Times in Canada, 2007." Available at www.hc-sc.gc.ca/hcs-sss/qual/acces/wait-attente/index-eng.php.

4 Barua, Rovere, and Skinner, pp. 29, 38.

5 Davis, Karen , et al. "Mirror, Mirror on the Wall: An International Update on the Comparative Performance of American Health Care," Commonwealth Fund. May 15, 2007.

6 Thompson, Erin. "Wait Times to See a Doctor Are Getting Longer," *USA Today.* June 3, 2009. Available at www.usatoday.com/news/health/2009-06-03-waittimes_N.htm.

7 When talking about healthcare, differentiating between wants and needs becomes both important and extremely difficult. Some people *need* care right away. Others simply don't want to wait when they visit a doctor to ask a few questions. Separating these two groups is but one of the major challenges faced by those providing care and those seeking to regulate the industry.

ration a limited supply by raising the money price of a good or service, since the people who want or need it most should be willing to pay the highest price. But if you're uncomfortable relying on the price system to determine who gets access to medical care, you can "ration by waiting" (i.e., raise the time price). The assumption might be that this is more fair toward those with less money to spend—but, as the Canadians have learned, it can be less fair to those with less time to spend.

HEALTHCARE QUALITY AND ACCESS IN AMERICA

The issue of how America's healthcare system stacks up to our neighbors took center stage in 2009 as President Obama pushed for the passage of his healthcare reforms. At the time, some surveys ranked the United States' system dead last against those in six other countries, including Canada. The untold story here is that these surveys based their rankings not so much on, say, cancer survival rates or access to the latest medicines but on things like "equity" (how cheap or widely available care is) and "healthy living" (the diet, exercise, and lifestyle choices we make).[8] Small wonder that we came last in a contest stacked against the very principles on which our system is built: high quality care and freedom of choice.

But making healthcare available to everyone "for free" might make a system only *theoretically* more equitable. At a zero price, more will be demanded but may or may not be supplied. As Canada shows, making care more affordable doesn't guarantee it'll be available—at least not in a timely fashion. And as for "healthy living," often good health is a result of personal choices. People base their daily decisions on the array of options available and on the potential consequences of choosing each one. Unfortunately, Americans are not known for making healthy choices or for having a long-term outlook—and we're not alone in this, as you will see.

THE FRENCH CONNECTION

I started my own informal study of this topic during the semester I spent studying in France, a country with a healthcare system similar to Canada's. I had a lot of good talks with French people about their system, which was rated the best in the world by the World Health Organization in 2001. Yet many of these conversations devolved into complaints about their so-called number-one healthcare system. Now, the French love to complain—almost as much as I do—and my sample of acquaintances was

---

8 Gratzer, David, and Matthews, Merrill. "Last in Credibility," *The Weekly Standard*. August 16, 2010. Available at www.weeklystandard.com/articles/last-credibility. The National Center for Policy Analysis points out that the United States has the highest rates for 5-year cancer survival when compared with Europe and that Americans also have a better chance of survival than our neighbors to the north in Canada. For their 2007 study, visit www.ncpa.org/pub/ba596.

completely unscientific, so I can't say my experiences are necessarily the norm, but the fact remains: The great majority of those I talked to about healthcare in France had one objection or another.

There was one old Frenchman with whom I spoke at length in a café (while he smoked a pipe in blatant disregard of the "no smoking indoors" law, which had recently passed) who summed up what I had heard a number of times before with one wish: that president Nicholas Sarkozy would "Americanize" France's failing system. He cited long wait times and inaccessible doctors, among other concerns.

It's okay. I was a little surprised, too.

It was also interesting to see who did *not* complain about the French system. Those who seemed happiest about the "free" (taxpayer funded) healthcare were the "clochards"—twenty-somethings who often (but not always) *choose* to be homeless. They spend their days begging for spare change, which they use to buy tobacco, cheap beer, and kabobs. Since they have the healthcare buffet as a fallback, they don't exactly need to set aside any extra for doctor's visits or emergency surgery.

In a similar display of irresponsibility, my less-than-well-off host in the south of France, who had already suffered through cancer twice, continued smoking and drinking as only a Frenchwoman can. Why? Apart from the natural human tendency to overindulge, access to "free" fixes can lead to irresponsible behavior. No matter what happens, she knows she'll have the healthcare buffet when things go wrong. By trying to seal up the cracks so people won't keep slipping through, France has created other problems.

Human behavior is not fixed or given; we respond to incentives. When the government pays for our cancer treatments and other health-care needs, it is effectively encouraging smoking and other risky behavior.

To learn more lessons about irresponsibility, however, I had only need to come home.

PEOPLE MAKING BAD DECISIONS

My buddy Tim is (as I write) 22 years old, rides a motorcycle, and works an average of 70 hours a week as a tow truck driver. He usually takes home well over $1,000 per week after taxes and, judging from the stories he has about getting threatened and even assaulted by disgruntled "clients," he earns every penny of it. He is also still one month away from completing his 6-month probationary period before he gets health benefits at work.

We have an invention for people like Tim. It's called COBRA insurance.[9] It could have provided him coverage during the 6 months between

---

9 COBRA stands for the Consolidated Omnibus Budget Reconciliation Act of 1985, which requires that most employers with group health plans offer employees the opportunity to temporarily continue their group healthcare coverage under their employer's plan if their coverage otherwise would cease due to termination, layoff, or other change in employment status.

the date he left his old job as a mechanic and the date he starts receiving benefits at his new one. But, with the wisdom that most twenty-some-things possess, Tim opted out of paying for temporary insurance, instead deciding to buy a $1,500 ignition setup for the race car he's building in his spare time. He's rolling the dice, gambling that he won't have an accident and need expensive medical treatment—or that if he does, someone else (his parents or taxpayers) will foot the bill.[10]

Unfortunately, my friends aren't the only ones making short-sighted decisions. Like a lot of other folks these days, my barber recently found his business in a tough spot, and, to stay afloat, he stopped paying for health insurance for his family. Later that month, he bought his daughter that pony she's always wanted for her birthday. Now she's riding around on a pony and is not even covered in the event of an accident.[11] Sound familiar? But Tim personally chose to gamble on his own good health so he could spend his money on other stuff. This little girl had the bad deci-sion thrust upon her.

What, my fellow humans, is the appropriate response to all of this? We're all generally good people, and we're simply not okay with letting others suffer just because they're short on cash or judgment. Healthcare is a funny thing. Some of us can pay for it, some of us can't, and some who can pay for it *choose* not to—but nearly everyone will need it sooner or later. So is free healthcare really a bad thing?

"Free" Lunches and Behavior

What have we learned from our look into healthcare in Canada and France, two countries that have based their systems on the idea that pay-ing for medical care is an act so immoral that it should be reserved only for the government?

First, we shouldn't really call their systems free because, obviously, there is no such thing. "There's no free lunch" is such a cliché among economists that nearly everyone is familiar with it.[12] The basic idea is that when we're given something at a price of $0.00, that doesn't mean it

---

10 Taking risks in the expectation that you'll get to keep any resulting benefits while others will pay if you don't win your gamble is called "moral hazard," which you might have heard of in connection with the recent shenanigans on Wall Street. But it's also relevant to the healthcare market. For example, since it's illegal in the United States to deny someone care in a hospital emergency room (even if he or she cannot pay for it), people sometimes forego insurance and use emergency rooms if they get sick, passing the cost of their healthcare along to the hospital, who then passes it on to taxpayers or to insurance companies, who then pass it on to those who can afford to pay for insurance.

11 I'm not making this up: a pony instead of health insurance. When I was doing research for my first motorcycle, I ran across a statistic that claimed that there are more injuries per hour spent on horseback than riding a motorcycle, although I am sure the severity differs greatly.

12 Anyone seen the acronym TINSTAAFL? It stands for "There is no such thing as a free lunch," of course! Think of it as the economists' version of WWJD?

costs $0.00 to produce. *Someone* pays those costs. Someone *always* pays—though often the payments are disguised.

The "free" healthcare those Canadians and French depend on must get paid for somewhere along the line, even if a check isn't written at the doctor's office. Taxpayers, of course, pay a large portion of the bill, although few of them stop and think about how many hours per day they're working to pay their medical bills in this roundabout way. But tax dollars are just part of the equation: As we've seen, when the price of an extra "plateful" from the healthcare buffet is nothing, much more care might be demanded than is supplied, and that mismatch is resolved by waiting.

If you've got a bad knee and can't work for 9 months because your orthopedic surgeon has a huge waitlist, that's pretty costly. The Fraser Institute study (mentioned earlier) calculated that on any given day almost 2.5 percent of Canadians are waiting for needed medical treatment, and economists have estimated that the average "waiting cost per patient" is anywhere from $859 to $2,628 (depending on how the value of lost work or leisure time is measured).[13] So you might hear that other countries spend considerably less on healthcare than we do in the United States, but it's worth remembering that some of their costs are hidden in this way.

A second issue is quality. Whenever my fellow regulars and I went to the Great Fortune Chinese Buffet, we'd head straight for the good stuff—the shrimp, beef, or chicken dishes—and ignore the menu items that cost the owner less to produce. That, of course, put pressure on the owner's profit margins, and he responded by sneaking more broccoli and water chestnuts into his recipes (and, as I mentioned, cutting back on the visits by the exterminator). Similar—but obviously much more important—cutbacks in quality might happen in the medical care industry when we try to accommodate more patients wanting more services with a limited budget. And that might account for some of my French friends' complaints about their system.

In any case, although we Americans pay a lot for our medical care, we also get care that is, on average, excellent. A recently published comparison of cancer survival rates for almost 2 million patients in 31 countries found that, for 16 types of cancer studied, American men have a survival rate of 66 percent versus only 47 percent for European men, and American women have a 63 percent survival rate versus 56 percent for Europeans. Survival rates are 90 percent or higher for five types of cancer in the United States but for only one in Europe.[14]

---

13 Barua, Rovere, and Skinner, p. 29.
14 Coleman, Michel P., et al., "Cancer Survival in Five Continents: A Worldwide Population-Based Study (CONCORD)." *The Lancet Oncology*, vol. 9, no. 8 (August, 2008), pp. 730–756. As cited by Gratzer and Matthews.

There's a reason not all restaurants are buffets. Paying by the plateful is clearly the best way to keep customers from overdoing it.[15] And paying different prices for steak than for noodles is the best way to ensure that steak is available. Maybe our American system is not as broken as it seems.

Wouldn't it be nice, though, if we could combine the quality and choice of the U.S. system with lower costs and greater access? That is, surely, the hope of President Obama and those who advocated the Patient Protection and Affordable Care Act (PPACA) he signed into law in March 2010. Clearly, a full discussion of that legislation—which ran over 2,000 pages—is way beyond the scope of this chapter.

But some of the PPACA's key provisions relate directly to the kinds of behavior I described earlier. Not just the short-sighted choices made by the "clochards" and my host in France but also the gambles taken by people like my buddy Tim and my barber.

PEOPLE ARE LIKE PORSCHES—OR HONDAS

Any parent will tell you the importance of establishing boundaries and consequences for overindulgence and harmful behavior. On the other hand, learning the consequences of riding a motorcycle or smoking a pack of cigarettes every day can be costly, and we're generally not okay with watching someone go without healthcare just to teach him or her a lesson, valuable though it may be. So before we take on the topic of what to do about people who can't afford healthcare, let's ask a harder question: What do we do about those (like Tim) who can afford insurance but choose not to buy it?

I hope by now I've made a case that the "use tax money and make healthcare 'free' for everybody" strategy creates problems of its own. But you can't opt out of paying taxes, so this approach seems to ensure that Tim will both get care if he needs it and actually contribute toward its costs. Yet remember the waiting lists in Canada, the quality issues in Europe, and the behavioral responses to "free" care from people like my chain-smoking host. Before long, we might have just as many complaints about our healthcare buffet as the French.

Consider, on the other hand, how we handle car insurance.

We buy insurance against damage to (or theft of) our cars because there are lots of crazy people out there who we don't trust. What if they back into us in a parking lot and dent our door? Or, T-bone us in an intersection and break our legs? Most of us recognize that these risks are significant and would voluntarily insure against their costs, but because some people make short-sighted choices we have laws *mandating* that

---

15 Without this tactic at their disposal, some buffets have to ban their biggest clients, if you know what I mean.

everyone buys insurance before they get on the road. This is partly to prevent the costs of accidents involving uninsured drivers from falling on their victims. But it's also because, without making insurance compulsory, bad drivers (who know they're more likely to have an accident and get their repairs paid for) might be more likely to buy insurance than great drivers (who gamble that they can avoid accidents in the first place).[16] The more times this happens, the higher rates have to be for everybody else, which can create a downward spiral in which fewer and fewer people decide it's worthwhile to buy insurance and eventually no one has it but the rich and the reckless.

Although we've made car insurance compulsory, we've decided not to make it free (i.e., paid for by taxpayers), uniform across all buyers ("one size fits all"), or the exclusive domain of a single payer (a government enterprise). And no one I know suggests we do otherwise. It makes sense for the driver of an expensive Porsche to pay more for collision or theft coverage than the driver of a practical Honda, for drivers who have lots of accidents to pay more for coverage than those who are more careful, and for competition among insurers to keep overhead under control and rates as low as feasible.

In other words, the car insurance market works reasonably well because it's *not* an all-you-can-eat buffet. But to work as well as it does requires one key regulation that makes the insurance pool as large as possible.

Now, driving might be one of the most dangerous things we ever do, but is our health really that much more predictable than our fate on the highways? Why not just require people to buy health insurance if they want to leave their house, just like we require them to insure their vehicles if they want to leave the garage?

THE PATIENT PROTECTION AND AFFORDABLE CARE ACT

In case you missed it, we *did* make health insurance coverage compulsory in the PPACA (which, yes, most people call "Obamacare"). And those who choose to ignore that mandate are supposed to be subjected to penalties. The basic idea was not just to broaden the insurance pool by getting people like my buddy Tim (so far, a healthy specimen) to pay into it but also to head off possible unwholesome behavior arising from the PPACA's solution to another problem: the fact that most health insurance companies won't give you coverage for preexisting conditions.

You can understand why the companies say no in such cases. If you could, say, break your arm and *then* buy the insurance policy that would pay for your X-rays, cast, and doctor visits, you'd never buy insurance

---

16 This taps into the economic concept of "adverse selection," because when a careful driver chooses not to buy insurance the size of the insurance pool shrinks and costs rise for everyone else.

and pay *into* the pool until you needed to draw even more *out* of it. That wouldn't work any better than a car insurance system where you could call Geico and get coverage right after a fender bender and then drop the policy as soon as the repairs were done and paid for (by them).

Telling insurers they'd have to start covering preexisting conditions was one of the more popular parts of the PPACA. Without that change, many Americans found themselves unable to change jobs (and insurers), and others couldn't get coverage at all. But the preexisting condition clause needs the compulsory coverage clause as a partner. It has to be a package deal, or you're inviting people to game the system.

Unfortunately, lots of people don't see compulsory health insurance in the same benign way they see compulsory auto insurance. Almost as soon as the law was signed, more than half the states sued to block implementation of the individual mandate provision, and as this is written it's impossible to predict how this is going to be resolved: some lower courts have said this element of the PPACA is unconstitutional, others have said it's fine, and the issue is before the Supreme Court—perhaps even decided by the time this is published.

But, of course, a 2,000-plus-page law aims to do a lot more than get everyone to buy insurance coverage. Many new stipulations about the types of care that need to be covered by all insurance plans (think "menu items added to the buffet table") will serve to increase the cost of coverage and might place many consumers in an awkward middle ground where we pay not just for what we want but also are forced to buy things we do not.

A Separate Issue

Of course, there will always be the unfortunate poor who can't afford to buy health insurance, no matter how carefully we design coverage plans or how much we expand the insurance pool through an individual mandate. But it's important to recognize that this is a problem of poverty and not necessarily an indictment of the health insurance or healthcare-delivery industries.

Economists warn that it's much better to deal with poverty by transferring income to the poor, whether in cash or in kind, than by tinkering with price controls or regulations we think will enable the poor to buy what they need (or what we think they should want). That's why, for example, we have a food stamp program to alleviate hunger rather than a law that says bread must sell for a nickel. We know the latter would simply cause bakers to find a new line of work.

We increase the poor's access to healthcare with Medicaid, which pays some or all medical costs for those who have low incomes and meet certain other eligibility requirements. The PPACA expands Medicaid eligibility to individuals and families with incomes up to 133 percent of the poverty level. What's more, low-income individuals and families not eligible for

Medicaid but with incomes up to four times the poverty threshold are now eligible for subsidies (which get smaller as their incomes rise) if they choose to purchase insurance from newly created insurance "exchanges" created by states.

Subsidies like these pose what is sometimes called the "Samaritan's dilemma." We want to be good Samaritans and help those in need, but sometimes the knowledge that there is help available encourages those getting aid not to do things—like invest in education or work more hours (remember those clochards?)—that would make them better off. What's more, the subsidies must come from somewhere, and our judgment about whether the subsidies are fair or just must take into account who bears their costs.

There are, naturally, many who believe that the PPACA doesn't go far enough to increase access to healthcare and that a single-payer system (like those in France or Canada) is really just "compulsory insurance" that would be cheaper than any private carrier could or would offer. These folks must have more faith in big government—and less in the efficiencies and cost savings that typically arise from market competition—than I do.

In any case, the PPACA didn't go nearly that far, though it did invite many more people to the healthcare buffet and played around with the buffet's menu and pricing—without, however, bringing out more food (i.e., increasing the supply of doctors or other healthcare suppliers). Whether we'll consider these changes tasty or not is a question for whoever writes the cryptic messages in fortune cookies; we won't have a definitive answer for many years down the road.

READ ON/JOIN UP

➢ We all read this book before we started work on *Econversations* because it is a great example of what a "fun" economics book should be. More than that, however, the author devotes a chapter to talking about healthcare, using Singapore's national system as an example of what we may want to consider for this country:

Harford, Tim. *The Undercover Economist: Exposing Why the Rich Are Rich, the Poor Are Poor—And Why You Can Never Buy a Decent Used Car!* Oxford, UK: Oxford University Press, 2005.

➢ My doctor recommended this book to me the last time I saw him for a check-up:

Potter, Wendell. *Deadly Spin: An Insurance Company Insider Speaks Out on How Corporate PR Is Killing Health Care and Deceiving Americans.* New York: Bloomsbury Press, 2010.

➢ For quick links to the Web sites discussed below, please visit www. pearsonhighered.com/walters:

There is an ongoing project of the Wall Street Journal, which can be an excellent resource for sound research and commentary on the state of healthcare in America and abroad today.

Check out another great healthcare blog, the Healthcare Blog—reading this regularly along with the WSJ blog should provide a more balanced perspective.

For those who want to stay up-to-date on the PPACA and Obamacare, ObamaCare Watch may be a good resource.

Questions for Discussion

1. "All-you-can-eat pricing" doesn't just occur at buffet restaurants: Identify some other examples of goods that you can buy for a single, up-front payment that allows "unlimited" consumption or usage. What problems, if any, arise from such pricing in the examples you named?

2. Think of a situation in your own life where you have encountered a "moral hazard" problem. Specifically, what was the risk that you faced, what were the benefits you would have obtained if you had taken that risk, and who would have paid the costs if you had taken the risk and lost your gamble? Did you take that risk? Why or why not?

3. The constitutionality of the "individual mandate" (i.e., compulsory insurance) that is part of the PPACA is a matter for legal scholars to debate and the Supreme Court to decide. What are the economic problems that the mandate is supposed to solve, and how does it solve them? Can you think of any alternative ways to address these issues (focusing on economics, rather than politics or the law)?

4. Government-financed healthcare programs like Medicaid and Medicare are getting expensive as the population in the United States ages. Since total government expenditures for such programs equals the price paid per doctor visit or procedure times the number of such visits or procedures, sometimes the government chooses to reduce its expenditures by reducing the prices it will pay per visit or procedure. What effects will this have on the amount of healthcare supplied? Why? How will this affect patients covered by these programs? How will they adapt?

5. Healthcare costs are rising steadily in this country. Do you find yourself worrying about how you will afford health insurance when you are older? What possible solutions would you propose to combat the ever-increasing costs? Are there any alternatives you hear other individuals or groups proposing that seem reasonable?

CHAPTER 7

Green Is the New Black

Environmental Problems and Policy

by Nicholas L. Centanni

The college idealists who fill the ranks of the environmental movement seem willing to do absolutely anything to save the biosphere, except take science courses and learn something about it.

—P. J. O'ROURKE

Chapter Highlights

- The Tragedy of the Commons
- The Coase Theorem
- Negative and Positive Externalities
- Environmental Regulation
- Cost-Benefit Analysis

Yelling is a time-tested way of getting attention. Yelling something outrageous? Even better.

That must have been the strategy of the impassioned volunteer at the information table outside the campus cafeteria. Her high-decibel, apocalyptic message to seemingly uninterested students trying to make it to classes that started 5 minutes ago went like this: "The world is going to end in 2012 if we don't do something to stop global warming!"[1]

She had me at "the world is going to end." I hustled over to ask for details on our exact expiration date so I could plan accordingly. Unfortunately, she sensed the sarcasm in my tone and was not amused. I tried to seem more sympathetic. I really *did* want to know what she was promoting.

---

1 If you're reading this after 2012, you should (a) be happy and (b) know that "doomsday" predictions about the world ending that year were common. There was even a movie about it. Many said that there was a direct link between environmental inaction and the world coming to an end.

Her goal, she explained warily, was to get fellow students like me to petition the government "so we can all live in a better world."

Well, sure, I thought. Who's against a better world? And governments have a great track record of getting that done, whether it involves big matters like war and peace or small ones like carrying a letter across town in less than 3 days. Oh, shoot—did I say that out loud? Oops.

The volunteer frowned, told me to put the global warming pamphlet I'd just picked up right back on the table where I'd found it, and turned her attention to someone at the other end of her table—someone more truly sympathetic. Note to self: Take the snarkiness down a notch. Man, what's my problem? I'm just as concerned as the next guy about the environment and making people's lives better. But instead of having a nice chat about our impending doom and signing a petition that would help save us all, here I was getting the cold shoulder.

THE WORLD CAFETERIA

Just before getting brushed off by the global warming activist, I'd been studying for my econ midterm in the cafeteria. I'd arrived early in the morning so I could stake out a prime spot by a window and minimize distractions, and I was making good progress reviewing an article titled "The Problem of Social Cost," by a Nobel Prize–winning economist named Ronald Coase. Then it happened: Some "loud talkers" sat down at the table next to me.

They chattered away nonstop and at high volume. Which meant that my poor brain got confusing messages. Economics got crowded out by the latest gossip about various students. I was definitely affected by their conversation even though I was no part of it. And there was nothing I could do. I mean, a cafeteria is a place where it's just as legitimate to socialize as it is to sip coffee and read quietly. I had no right to tell them to stop talking, and they had no right to tell me to stop studying.

So maybe that's why I was so grumpy when I had the chance to help save the world. I was probably worried that on my exam I'd answer a question about Ronald Coase with, "I'm pretty sure he's the dude that someone named Courtney dumped last weekend."

Eventually, though, I calmed down and put things together. Everything I'd been doing that morning was actually related—and it all dealt with something economists call the "tragedy of the commons." The basic problem is that when everybody owns something—that is, when it's "common property"—there are inevitable conflicts about how to use it. Often, those conflicts can lead to the degradation or destruction of the property itself. For example, socializers make the cafeteria less useful for studying—or if studiers lay a guilt trip on socializers and make them quiet down, then the place is less useful for that. How it all works out is bound to be annoying to one group or the other. But when we're talking about bigger issues, like using the atmosphere as a "commons," and some people want to breathe it while others want to use it to dispose of pollutants, then the outcome of this conflict could be tragic.

They're really examples of the same problem, though. The fact that I was affected by the other students' conversation was a "spillover cost" or, in econ-speak, a "negative externality" (because I was "external" to their transaction—that is, conversation). It's just a more serious externality problem when I breathe air that you might have polluted by driving your car or turning on your lights.[2]

But here's the key thing: *Everyone* wants to solve these problems and resolve these conflicts. I do, the volunteer with the global warming petition does, and you do. What's apparent from the often-heated debate about these issues, though, is that there's a lot of disagreement about which problems need to be solved first and how best to do that. In this short chapter, we can't address all of the disagreements people have about environmental policy—or even many of them—but we can identify a few basic principles that we need to agree on if we're going to have a civilized discussion about environmental issues.

EVERYTHING COSTS SOMETHING

Here's a question for you: How much poorer are you willing to be to enjoy a cleaner environment? Are you willing to sacrifice 5 percent of your income for this laudable goal? Fifty percent? More? People will have different preferences about this, just like some people are willing to spend $300 for a really nice pair of shoes while others always shop at the Discount Shoe Barn and never pay more than $50, preferring to spend their money on other stuff. But we all need to acknowledge that more environmental quality is likely to cost *something*—that, as the old cliché has it, "There's no such thing as a free lunch."

Most people get this. But quite a few of us think we can enjoy the lunch by simply getting someone else to pick up the tab. As one of my friends remarked when we were discussing the costs of many environmental programs, "Well, the government can just tax the big businesses who can afford to pay for it instead of us." Of course, that doesn't make the programs "free" to society—and it may not get us off the hook, either.

For example, suppose you run a company that makes sprockets. Any profits you earn each year are either (a) sent to the stockholders who supplied you with the capital you needed to get into the business or (b) plowed back into the company for new equipment, better technology,

---

2 Of course, there can be spillover benefits, or positive externalities, too. If the conversation at the next table had started out, "Last night my econ tutor explained all the key stuff we need to know about Coase...," I would have been all ears. Or, if you plant some trees, I breathe cleaner air.

or more workers that will enable you to remain among the top sprocket makers in the country. If some or all of those profits are taxed away, your disappointed stockholders will look for better investments and you'll be starved for capital. Or you'll be less competitive because you don't have as much money for equipment, R&D, or labor. Or you'll try to restore those lost profits by raising prices to consumers,[3] and they push back by buying less sprockets. No free lunch.

Costs Are Never Irrelevant

Another problem is that a lot of people seem to think that costs don't matter. Here's a scary result from an opinion survey by the Harris polling organization: In 2005, 74 percent of Americans agreed with the statement that "protecting the environment is so important that requirements and standards cannot be too high, and continuing improvements must be made regardless of cost."[4]

I'm going to go out on a limb here. I suspect most people weren't listening by the time the pollster got to that last part. We all want to be identified as good people, and good people nod in agreement when we're asked if the environment's important, whether improvements must be made, bla bla—and the "regardless of cost" sneaks right by us. If we're paying close attention, we say, "Uh, no way. I'm not willing to give up, say, half my income for a 1 percent improvement in air quality. That 'regardless' is a deal breaker."

I could be wrong, but I'm suggesting that most people—if a poll question were actually to become real-life environmental policy—would be very reluctant to give anybody an unlimited budget for anything, even something as wonderful as cleaner air or water. People don't like to pay more for something than it's worth—which is to say we generally compare benefits to costs when we're making decisions. And that's smart, whether we're talking about policies that affect millions of people or just a few.

I would also argue that it's smart to be *realistic* about your estimates of benefits and costs when you're making decisions. If your mind's already made up, it'll be tempting to exaggerate on one side or the other—to yell, for example, that not doing something right now will cause the world to end in a couple of years. Saving the world is obviously a nice benefit, and

---

3 Note that the burden of most taxes we impose on businesses will be *shared* by the businesses themselves (or their stockholders) and the consumers of their products. Taxes increase their costs, and they may try to pass all of these increased costs on to consumers, but they're usually unsuccessful in doing so, because consumers respond to higher prices by buying less.

4 As cited in Teixeira, Ruy. "What the Public Really Wants on Energy and the Environment." Center for American Progress. March 5, 2007. Available at www.americanprogress.org/issues/2007/03/wtprw.html.

most of us would be happy to pay a fairly steep cost to do it. But exaggerations can lead to bad decisions—and once they're found out, they'll damage our credibility and maybe keep us from convincing people to do good things in the future.

ONE SIZE DOES NOT FIT ALL

Even when we decide to impose regulations that might generate greater benefits than costs, we have to be careful about how we do it. Sometimes we can make regulations operate better by recognizing the diversity among people (or businesses) and leaving it to them to figure out how to improve the environment most cheaply and effectively.

Suppose, for example, that after careful study we conclude that cutting energy use by 10 percent would lead to environmental improvements of greater value than the lost output of goods and services resulting from the lower energy use. One way to do this is to give everybody a fixed "energy allowance"—maybe by looking at our electric and gas bills, seeing how many kilowatt hours of electricity or cubic feet of natural gas we used last year, and telling us we'll be shut off when we hit 90 percent of that figure this year.

Sounds fair. Treats us all alike, whether rich or poor, young or old. But we're obviously *not* all alike, and treating us as if we are might be both unfair and unnecessarily expensive. Your grandma, for example, might be very sensitive to the cold and horrified at the prospect of turning her thermostat down several degrees. Instead, she'd pay handsomely to stay warm. You, on the other hand, are the type to wear shorts even in the winter. You'd gladly turn your thermostat *way* down—if grandma makes it worth your while. A more flexible regulatory regime that allows grandma to buy the right to keep her thermostat where she likes it in exchange for your willingness to cut your consumption 20 percent—which is better known as a "cap and trade" system—can get society to the desired, lower energy consumption level without as much misery as the across-the-board approach would cause.[5]

Or, if we're talking about businesses instead of individuals, letting firms trade permits to use energy or pollute can minimize the costs of a particular regulation. If we just say, "Everybody has to cut pollution by 10 percent, no exceptions," and ignore the fact that some companies might be able to cut their pollution levels more cheaply than others, we'll

---

5 In fact, the Environmental Protection Agency already uses something like this system to control pollution cost effectively in many areas. For example, under its "offset" policy, emissions of some pollutants within certain boundaries are capped. If a new company wants to enter that market and its operations would add to pollution problems, it would need to buy offsetting reductions in emissions from existing firms. Obviously, it could only afford to do so if the value of its output significantly exceeded that of the companies it bought out—much like grandma valuing warmth more than you.

spend a lot more money than necessary to achieve that goal. Some, like grandma, might find it very expensive to meet an across-the-board quota, while others might be able to exceed the average pollution reduction at relatively low cost. Why not reward the latter by allowing them to sell their "surplus" reductions to those in need?[6] You'll hit your target, save some resources, and kick off some healthy competition to figure out more cost-effective ways to avoid pollution.

Ideas Have Consequences—and Side Effects

I like to eat off clean dishes. Luckily, some brilliant chemists figured out that putting phosphates in dish soap makes it real easy to remove grease and get plates squeaky clean. There's only one problem: The suds that go down the drain eventually end up in nearby bodies of water, and those phosphates promote algae growth that blocks sunlight, makes it hard for plants to grow in that water, and ultimately reduces fish populations.[7]

After seeing this happen in their area, elected officials in Spokane, Washington, passed a law banning the sale of soap containing phosphates. Pollution problem solved! Except, unfortunately, the replacement soap didn't work nearly as well as the soap with phosphates. In fact, most people found they needed to set their dishwashers to a higher setting or use a longer wash cycle, which ultimately led to using more energy and water.

So there was an unexpected side effect of the new law: Less phosphate runoff improved water quality in some areas, but slightly higher energy and water consumption gave some of those environmental benefits back in other areas. Nevertheless, Spokane decided that using more water and energy was the optimal route.

But wait, there's more. When something is banned, an "underground market" often arises. Even for soap. In Spokane, soon after the soap ban, there were reports of people driving to nearby Idaho, stocking up on soap with phosphates, and bringing it back home.[8] The things people will do for clean dishes (and, apparently, when people tell pollsters

---

6 Suppose, for example, that Coke can reduce its air pollution emissions for $1 per ton, while it costs Pepsi $2 per ton (for reasons we don't need to get into). If we require each company to cut emissions 10 tons, the total cost of this 20-ton reduction is $30. If, instead, Coke did it all, the cost of the same amount of environmental improvement would be only $20, a saving of one-third. But it might seem unfair to punish Coke for being more efficient at "being green," so we could get the same result by having Pepsi buy its 10-ton reduction from Coke for, say, $1.50 per. Pepsi saves money, Coke profits from its superior efficiency, and the world gets cleaner—all thanks to another variation on cap and trade.

7 This is just another example of the negative externality problem we discussed earlier. We transact with the soap companies, but those external to our transactions—the fish and those who value them for sport or food, or anyone who values cleaner water—pay some costs as a result.

8 See Murphy, Kim. "The Dirty Truth: They're Smuggling Soap in Spokane." *Los Angeles Times.* April 6, 2009. Available at www.latimes.com/news/nationworld/nation/la-na-soap-smuggling6-2009apr06,0,3154007.story.

they'd pay any price for greater environmental quality, a lot of them don't really mean it). Anyway, the use of phosphate soaps by those willing to smuggle them into Spokane, plus the pollution they created driving to Idaho, gave away more of the expected environmental benefits of the law.

These kinds of unexpected side effects of regulations, which sometimes turn out to cause more problems than they were trying to solve, are pretty common. Another example: compact fluorescent lightbulbs (CFLs). They produce more light with less energy, and if they're used widely we can potentially cut greenhouse gas emissions. So, some countries are adopting regulations that will phase out old-fashioned, Edison-style lightbulbs and promote use of CFLs in their place.

But there's a hitch. Each CFL has a small amount of mercury in it, which is highly toxic. If you break a CFL, you have to be very careful not to breathe mercury vapor as you're cleaning it up, and you're supposed to dispose of CFLs at proper recycling centers.[9] By some estimates, though, only 20 percent of CFLs are recycled right now, so, again, we might be giving back some of the environmental benefits of CFL use in unexpected and unintended environmental or health costs.

This doesn't mean we should never regulate, or that we shouldn't bother with benefit-cost analysis as a way of making regulations work better. Just the opposite: We have to weigh benefits and costs even more carefully than we sometimes do and consider how people actually behave in the real world rather than how we hope they'll behave.

GREEN JOBS: THE KEY THAT UNLOCKS ALL?

Lately, "green jobs"[10] have been advertised as a twofer—a solution to both environmental and unemployment problems. As one of my friends put it, "When the government creates green jobs, unemployment decreases and we help solve global warming at the same time, so we have two benefits for every green job we create." And when she told me this, she seemed just as excited as that volunteer trying to avoid the end of the world.

---

9 For a good summary of how you're supposed to properly use and dispose of CFLs, see Matson, John. "Are Compact Fluorescent Lightbulbs Dangerous?" *Scientific American*. April 10, 2008. Available at www.scientificamerican.com/article.cfm?id=are-compact-fluorescent-lightbulbs-dangerous.

10 According to the United Nations Environment Program, a green job is defined as "Work in agricultural, manufacturing, research and development (R&D), administrative, and service activities that contribute(s) substantially to preserving or restoring environmental quality. Specifically, but not exclusively, this includes jobs that help to protect ecosystems and biodiversity; reduce energy, materials, and water consumption through high efficiency strategies; de-carbonize the economy; and minimize or altogether avoid generation of all forms of waste and pollution." See www.unep.org/labour_environment/PDFs/Greenjobs/UNEP-Green-Jobs-Report.pdf.

But it sounded a little too good to be true to me—like, double benefits, no costs? And upon further review, there are, unfortunately, costs associated with green jobs programs. European countries—Spain in particular—have been focused on creating green jobs longer than the United States has, so we can learn a lot from them. One study of Spain's experience concluded that for every renewable-energy job created by the government, there were 2.2 jobs *lost* in other sectors of the economy.[11]

How can a program to create jobs actually reduce employment? The key is that a lot of green jobs involve producing things at much higher cost than "nongreen" alternatives. Take wind power, for example. In the late 1990s, Spain started encouraging the production of renewable energy on "wind farms." Because it usually cost from one-third to one-half more (per kilowatt hour) to generate electricity with wind power than with more traditional (nonrenewable) methods, the Spanish government paid enormous subsidies to make firms willing and able to sell in this market. The aforementioned study estimated that these subsidies amounted to more than €1 million per green job created.[12] That money, raised via taxation that increased prices and reduced output of other goods and services, destroyed jobs elsewhere.

Again, that doesn't mean these kinds of programs are always unwise. Diverting some of our energy production from nonrenewable to renewable sources can yield major environmental benefits. All I'm saying is that we can't assume there will be no costs in the pursuit of those benefits; we have to do the benefit-cost analysis carefully if we really want to save the world.

THE POWER OF PROFIT

Here's another thing we should keep in mind as we try to solve environmental problems: Incentives matter, and it's usually a lot easier to get things done—and done right—when economic incentives are working *for* you rather than against you.

Most successful entrepreneurs made their fortunes either by figuring out something that people want that's not being produced yet or by selling at a lower cost something that others are already producing. They tend to be forward-looking—not fixated on just today but thinking about how to prosper in the future when there might be others who figure out how to do what they do better.

Take garbage collection, the ultimate in mundane industries. For many years, folks just carried their garbage to the curb and waited for it

11 See Calzada Alvarez, Gabriel, et al. "Study of the Effects on Employment of Public Aid to Renewable Energy Sources." Working paper. Universidad Rey Juan Carlos, March 2009. Available at www.juandemariana.org/pdf/090327-employment-public-aid-renewable.pdf.
12 Ibid., pp. 2, 9–12.

to be hauled to some far-off place. Then, thanks to new technologies, it became possible for some of our trash to be reused. Soon, many towns passed recycling laws requiring people to sort their trash—plastic in this bin, paper in that, plain old food scraps well, you know—so the reusable stuff wouldn't go into landfills and we wouldn't have to use so many resources to manufacture new plastic, paper, and so on. Unfortunately, though, there were a couple of problems. It was expensive to keep things separate (those pesky costs again), requiring towns to buy special trucks with numerous compartments and/or to make multiple pickups, so many areas were slow to get on board. And some found this process too time-consuming and messy for their busy lives and ignored the laws—even risking fines. So recycling programs weren't generating the environmental benefits they could.

But some entrepreneurs saw that there was money to be made if they could figure out how to cheaply sort out recyclables for us, at large-scale material-recovery facilities. One company called CP Manufacturing, for example, which had been profitably sorting and recycling scrap metals since the 1950s, turned its attention to paper, plastic, and other trash in the 1980s and opened its first co-mingled sorting system in Illinois by 1990; by the end of that decade, "single-stream recycling" was underway in several U.S. and Australian cities.[13] CP and other companies weren't doing this out of a sense of charity—they wanted to make a buck. But once they made it cheaper for cities to collect recyclables and for us to actually obey the recycling laws, the amount of trash recycled could increase. In other words, the profit motive helped accelerate environmental progress. Rules alone don't work as well as rules plus incentives.

Which makes me think about that Spokane soap example again. I remember in particular a *New York Times* story headlined "Exxon to Invest Millions to Make Fuel from Algae."[14] Hmm. To entrepreneurs, apparently, algae-choked water might be "green gold," useful in making things like biofuels, fertilizer, food products, or even in "algae bioreactors" that can reduce CO_2 emissions in power plants.[15] Now, I'm not saying we should deliberately pollute water using phosphate soap so we can harvest the resulting algae later. But maybe, from time to time, we need to think outside the box about how to deal with existing problems. That's what entrepreneurs are gifted at doing. As often as possible, then, we ought to conduct environmental policy in a way that harnesses incentives to get people to apply their creativity to pollution problems.

---

13 For more on the history of CP Manufacturing, see www.cpmfg.com/aboutus-history.html.

14 Mouawad, Jad. "Exxon to Invest Millions to Make Fuel from Algae." *New York Times.* July 14, 2009. Available at www.nytimes.com/2009/07/14/business/energy-environment/14fuel.html.

15 Oilgae. "Uses of Algae as Energy Source, Fertilizer, Food, and Pollution Control." Available at www.oilgae.com/algae/use/use.html.

GETTING BEYOND FEAR AND FASHION

So, believe it or not, I really want to "be green." My problem is that I have a tough time relating to people—like my fellow student yelling about the end of the world—who recruit followers by making people afraid or by trying to make it uncool not to be in their camp. Fear and fashion both have short lifespans; facts and reason are better motivators in the long run.

For example, if that global warming volunteer had been in college back in 1975, there's a good chance she would have been yelling about how the world was going to end if we didn't do something to stop global *cooling*: The April 28, 1975, edition of *Newsweek* predicted that declining temperatures around the globe soon would lead to, among other things, a catastrophic decrease in food production.[16] Another apocalyptic scenario was laid out by Paul Ehrlich in a 1968 book titled *The Population Bomb*, in which he predicted that as a result of overpopulation, "[i]n the 1970s and 1980s hundreds of millions of people will starve to death in spite of any crash programs embarked upon now. At this late date nothing can prevent a substantial increase in the world death rate."[17] Go back even further, to 1922, and the U.S. Geological Survey warned people that "[oil] reserves are enough to satisfy the present requirements of the United States for only 20 years, if the oil could be taken out of the ground as fast as it is wanted."[18]

Of course, we didn't run out of oil in 1942, we somehow avoided worldwide famine in the 1980s, and our fears of global cooling are long forgotten. That doesn't mean global warming isn't a problem—but it does mean that getting people to work toward practical solutions might be tougher, thanks to the track record of earlier prophets of gloom and doom.

And if we're going to make sustained progress on the environmental front, "being green" has to be more than just a fad. As one of my more fashion-conscious friends explained to me once, some styles come and go in a matter of months, but basic black is always in vogue. That's what we have to do with environmental awareness: make it of enduring value—which is much more likely if it's based on solid science, careful economics, and an entrepreneurial spirit dedicated to innovation.

READ ON/JOIN UP

➢ In one of the most famous papers about destroying the environment, Mr. Hardin speaks to how lack of ownership leads to overuse of resources: Hardin, G. "The Tragedy of the Commons." *Science*, 2000, vol. 162, no. 3859, pp. 1243–1248.

---

16 Gwynne, Peter. "The Cooling World." *Newsweek*. April 28, 1975, p. 64.
17 Ehrlich, Paul R. *The Population Bomb*. Cutchogue, NY: Buccaneer Books, 1968, p. xi.
18 United States Geological Survey. "The Oil Supply of the United States." *Bulletin of the American Association of Petroleum Geologists*. vol. 6, no. 1 (January 1922), pp. 42–46.

➤ Ronald Coase introduced what is now known as the Coase theorem. This may be a difficult read at first, but once a firm grasp on the concept is attained, it is evident why this theorem was at odds with the "Pigouvian" system prevalent at the time:

> Coase, Ronald. "The Problem of Social Cost." *Journal of Law and Economics*, 1960, vol. 3, no. 1, pp. 1–44.

➤ This book provides a compilation of many economic studies that have been conducted to rebuke common misconceptions. Each "myth" is dissected in great detail so the reader can see the conventional wisdom and then read about how studies have disproved the myth through data compilation and analysis:

> Spulber, Daniel F. *Famous Fables of Economics: Myths of Market Failures*. Malden, MA: Blackwell, 2002.

➤ For a quick link to the Web site discussing the below article, please visit *www.pearsonhighered.com/walters*:

> Written shortly after the collapse of the Soviet Union, this article captures the environmental record of a society where property rights did not exist. This article also confirms the "tragedy of the commons" mentioned earlier. "Why Socialism Causes Pollution," from Freeman Online.

QUESTIONS FOR DISCUSSION

1. Identify some real-world examples of "commonly owned property," either in history or today. In your experience, is such property generally cared for better or worse than privately owned property? Why?

2. Do you believe cost is ever irrelevant? That is, that we should not consider it or try to measure it in making a decision? If so, in what circumstances? Some argue that cost is impossible to measure in many circumstances—when, for example, there is the risk of loss of human life. Nevertheless, we often take risks that involve possible loss of life: We drive cars, fly in planes, and take stressful or dangerous jobs. Are we making irrational choices when we do so? How do we weigh the benefits against the costs of such risky activities?

3. Some argue that across-the-board regulations requiring everyone to reduce pollution by the same amount (or proportion) are fairer than a "cap and trade" system. Different people might have different ideas about fairness, but suppose in this case people mean that it's fair that everyone should *bear the same burden* (or total cost) of making the environment cleaner. Refer back to the example discussed in footnote 6, where Coke can reduce its air pollution emissions for $1 per ton, while it costs Pepsi $2 per ton. Now suppose that, guided by this particular concept of fairness, we require Coke and Pepsi each to spend $10 reducing their emissions. Do you consider that fair? Would

it be efficient (i.e., would it minimize the cost of a certain amount of pollution reduction)? Explain your answers.

4. Environmental regulation undoubtedly affects your life in some ways with which you are familiar. For example, recycling policies affect us almost daily. Identify a particular regulation that affects you, and consider whether it is having some "unintended consequences" (similar to those identified for the Spokane soap law). What are the costs (or benefits) of these consequences?

5. Ronald Coase won a Nobel Prize for analyzing externality problems, explaining how negotiations between those involved might control such problems, and showing how legal rulings might best be made when such negotiations are impossible or unlikely. For example, in the cafeteria, Coase might have suggested that I go over to the loud talkers and negotiate a deal, maybe paying them to pipe down or go elsewhere. How easy (or hard) do you think it would be to reach an agreement in this case? Even if I had done so, what additional problems might I have faced?

CHAPTER 8

Santa, Inc.

Firm Decisions and the Pursuit of Profit

by Christopher D. Appel

Profit is not the legitimate purpose of business. The legitimate purpose of business is to provide a product or service that people need and do it so well that it's profitable.

—JAMES ROUSE[1]

Chapter Highlights

- Profit (Economic vs. Accounting)
- Predatory Pricing
- Monopoly
- Scale Economies and Diseconomies
- Price Fixing

Santa is in a league of his own when it comes to producing and delivering the stuff we love. Throughout the year, everyone's favorite bearded guy oversees the manufacture of the toys and games we thoughtfully preorder, and then he gives them all away on a single night. To the best of our knowledge, he has a factory somewhere near the North Pole, where he employs an army of hardworking elves. And thanks to his amazing team of reindeer, Santa's operation is global; he has no trouble distributing gifts to homes all over the world quickly and efficiently.

Of course, Santa only has the capacity to deliver the goods on that one day, a holiday, when his potential competitors are closed. Lucky for them they don't have to compete with him on the other 364 days a year. They could never beat his combination of convenience, quality, and price (cookies and milk for the Big Fella; a few carrots for the reindeer). If Santa did take them on, it might make us happy, but you can bet that the list of disgruntled competitors would be very, very long. It

---

1 Excerpt from C-SPAN's American Profile Interview: Life and Career of James Rouse, April 10, 1992. Copyright © 1992 by C-SPAN.

might include manufacturers, retailers, online stores, delivery companies like UPS or FedEx, and probably their unions.[2] Imagine the accusatory headlines:

> *Mom and Pop Are out of Business; Santa, Inc. Blamed*
>
> *Does Santa Have an Illegal Monopoly? Justice Department Investigates*
>
> *Jobs Outsourced to North Pole; Congress Promises to Act Soon*
>
> *Exploited Elves? Labor Department Subpoenas Pay Records*

But wait . . . you don't really have to imagine those accusations. You've seen similar headlines already—except they're usually about Wal-Mart, the world's largest retailer and a frequent target of criticism about anticompetitive conduct, predatory pricing, and brutal labor practices. Okay, they don't employ elves or give toys away, and they're headquartered in Arkansas rather than the Arctic, but you get the idea: For a lot of people, Wal-Mart is a symbol of everything that's wrong with modern business—and maybe with capitalism itself. But what is Wal-Mart, really? What has it actually done? And why don't we admire it? This chapter explores these and other questions, putting Wal-Mart's performance in perspective without ignoring some of the mistakes that have made it such a polarizing company.

MOM-AND-POP SHOPS

The most common criticism of Wal-Mart is that it destroys small businesses that can't compete with its ridiculously low prices. Sure, consumers like those prices, but what about jobs? Does Wal-Mart create them or destroy them when it rolls into town and the "little guys" close their doors? The answer is a little bit of both.[3]

But before we get into the details, we should first note that evaluating Wal-Mart solely on its employment effects is simplistic and, potentially, misleading. Job loss or job creation figures are incomplete measures of a company's overall contribution to society. It would probably be better to focus on how much we value what the company is producing compared to the resources it uses in the process. It wouldn't do society any good to have a lot of companies with big payrolls supplying us with stuff we don't want at prices we can't afford. But Wal-Mart's effect on employment is a hot topic, so let's go there.

---

2 I assume Santa could produce more than just kids' stuff if he wanted to. If you've been bad, for example, you get coal, so he obviously has a mining operation. As far as I'm concerned, Santa's capable of just about anything. But he probably limits his output so he doesn't overwork the elves.

3 See: Basker, Emek. "Job Creation or Destruction? Labor Market Effects of Wal-Mart Expansion." *Review of Economics and Statistics*, vol. 87, no. 1 (February 2005), pp. 174–183.

For the moment, let's embrace the popular image of small-town America. Let's visit Pleasantville, where the Smith family has been running the general store, the Joneses have operated the pharmacy, and the Browns have had a grocery store for as long as anyone can remember. Shopkeepers fly red, white, and blue flags above their entrances and know you by name. Children ride their bikes home from school, stopping by the general store for some candy and soda pop along the way. The folks in town are quite happy with the prices and products carried by the Smiths, Joneses, and Browns. Not that they have any choice about it, because there's simply no place else to shop.

One day a dark cloud looms over the town. People are heard whispering that something evil is in the air. Then it happens: A giant yellow smiley face rolls over the horizon and emits a blinding flash. For several minutes no one can see anything. When they finally regain their vision, they see something massive on the outskirts of town. In the middle of a vast parking lot is a huge blue building with "Wal-Mart Super Center" emblazoned above its sliding doors.

People wonder what brought this behemoth to their quiet little town. The curious and the brave cautiously approach the structure. Once inside, their fear gives way to awe: Almost every product they need is right here, in one place, and it's all absurdly cheap. Not just clothing, food, and pharmaceuticals, but a bank, auto parts, toys, electronics, and some things people in the town have never even seen before. Right there on the shelf is a year's supply of pickles for three bucks![4] Pleasantville will never be the same again.

The Smiths, Joneses, and Browns are very uneasy about this development. Wal-Mart's prices are much lower than theirs. Can they compete? At first they consider Wal-Mart's arrival a challenge. They've always taken pride in their work; they're not about to roll over. They try their best to get up-to-speed. They search for better, cheaper suppliers; they try to give their customers more personalized service; they think about remodeling so they can stock a bigger selection of merchandise. But they face an uphill battle.

Their stores' size and product selection is small; Wal-Mart's is enormous. Their suppliers drive a hard bargain; Wal-Mart's are eager to give their biggest client "volume discounts." They take inventory with a pencil and paper and get deliveries infrequently; Wal-Mart manages its inventory with computer and satellite networks that rival the space program, and its fleet of trucks makes sure they're rarely out of stock on any item. When the Smiths, Joneses, or Browns need cash, they go to the town bank, fill out a loan application, and cross their fingers; Wal-Mart, as a publicly traded company, has access to capital from all over the world.

Unable to find a way to match Wal-Mart's selection, convenience, and prices, the Smiths, Joneses, and Browns eventually throw in the towel.

---

4 See Fishman, Charles. *The Wal-Mart Effect*. London: Penguin, 2006, p. 79.

They've been suspicious that Wal-Mart keeps its prices *artificially* low, plotting to raise them once they become the dominant store in town. But that doesn't happen: Even after the Smiths, Joneses, and Browns close their doors, Wal-Mart's prices stay low.

What *does* happen is that the Smiths, Joneses, and Browns are out of work. But not for long. Sure, that behemoth outside town always seems to be hiring. Since the folks they put out of business are a little bitter about that, however, it's understandable that they don't even want to shop at Wal-Mart, much less work there. But it turns out that the dollars that are now being saved on clothing, meds, groceries, and lots of other things are free to go elsewhere. The town's economy is actually expanding, allowing the Smiths, Joneses, and Browns to start new businesses that eventually prove quite successful.

Careful academic research[5] on this issue finds that when a Wal-Mart arrives, retail employment in a county goes up by 100 jobs. Over the next few years, as the Smiths, Joneses, and Browns exit, about half this gain goes away. Further, Wal-Mart is so efficient at inventory management (that's partly why its prices are so low) that another 30 wholesale jobs disappear, too. But that means, on net, that Wal-Marts are job *creators* rather than job destroyers, in both the short and long runs.

Naturally, though, when Mom and Pop's shop goes belly up, we assume it's bad and search for someone to blame. Big companies like Wal-Mart are easy targets. Often, successful firms are accused of predatory pricing—the practice of selling a product at a price below its cost in the hope that will drive out the competition. Once rivals have been destroyed, it's assumed the predator will be able to recoup its investment (the losses it incurred while selling below cost) by raising prices to monopoly levels.[6]

These days, however, outfits like Wal-Mart compete with more than just small, local retailers. There are other "big box" companies like Target and Best Buy cutting costs and looking for market share, of course, but even more threatening are the Internet-based retailers like Amazon and eBay. Raise your prices above the competitive level and your customers are very likely to go home, log on, and click their way to a better deal.

In any case, if Wal-Mart is a job creator and not a predator or a monopoly, why do so many people have issues with them? We see the For

---

5 See Basker.

6 A monopoly can theoretically occur when only one company exists in a market. This lonely company is able to change the price of a product simply by producing more or less of it. Such a company will have a greater incentive to produce less and charge a higher price than it would if competitors existed. In this sense, true monopolies are pretty rare since an alternative can almost always be found either right now or sometime in the near future. A much more realistic scenario, referred to as imperfect competition, is briefly described in the next two paragraphs.

Rent signs in the stores that the Smiths, Joneses, and Browns used to operate and blame Wal-Mart for that. But we also tend to look right past the other businesses that have flourished because of the extra disposable income people now have thanks to Wal-Mart's bargains. We see the bad fallout and ignore the good. What's more, some people might actually wish they could pay the Smiths, Joneses, and Browns higher prices in exchange for a more personal or intimate shopping experience—but with Wal-Mart around, they might not have that chance. So it really should be no big surprise that Wal-Mart is unpopular despite generally favorable effects on prices and employment; in fact, we've seen this all before.

THE SONG REMAINS THE SAME

During the mid- to late 1800s, the U.S. oil industry was made up of hundreds of small-scale businesses trying to strike it rich by refining crude petroleum from western Pennsylvania into, mainly, "illuminating oil" or kerosene.[7] John D. Rockefeller's Standard Oil Company started out small, too, but grew rapidly and revolutionized the industry with aggressive cost cutting, technological innovation, and integration into almost all stages of the production process. Between 1869 and 1885, Rockefeller cut the price of kerosene from 30 cents a gallon to only 8 cents.[8] In short, Standard Oil was the Wal-Mart of its day.

Such low prices for a crucial commodity attracted customers by the millions, and over the years Standard Oil's share of national kerosene sales soared to 90 percent. As it grew, many of Standard's competitors went bankrupt—or were bought out by Rockefeller. They were suspicious about how he could sell kerosene so cheaply, and many accused him of pricing his product below cost to drive them out of business and dominate the market—in effect, inventing the predatory pricing argument that has been popular ever since.

In truth, a lot of behavior that looked anticompetitive simply reflected the reduced costs that resulted from Standard's large size (which economists refer to as scale economies) and efficiency. For example, Rockefeller was able to negotiate volume discounts with the railroads that shipped his product because Standard's substantial output allowed him to fill entire tank cars with kerosene on a regular schedule. His smaller rivals,

---

7 This no doubt cost a lot of candle makers their jobs—even before Thomas Edison invented the lightbulb. As we noted in Chapter 1, technological change often reduces employment in some sectors while increasing it in others.

8 Data for this section are from Armentano, Dominick T. *Antitrust and Monopoly: Anatomy of a Policy Failure* (2nd ed.). Oakland, CA: The Independent Institute, 1990, pp. 55–73. Note that since whale oil was also used in lamps, Rockefeller didn't just reduce employment among candle makers: He sometimes is credited (facetiously or not) with saving whales from being hunted to extinction since he made kerosene so cheap and abundant.

on the other hand, often shipped output by the barrel, which involved much higher handling expenses and transaction costs. The railroads saved money dealing with Rockefeller and passed some of their savings on to him. But competitors that couldn't qualify for such discounts considered this unfair.

In addition, its greater size and cash flow allowed Standard to invest in facilities that performed key functions that his rivals had to pay others to do and to fund research that steadily reduced production costs. The company often found ways to take byproducts that other refineries wasted and convert them into new products and sources of revenue. And Standard integrated up and down the chain of production: It found new sources of crude oil, pumped it out of the ground, moved it to its refineries over its own pipelines, maintained a tanker fleet to reach distant markets, and employed a team of chemists who constantly sought ways to get more from less.[9]

In at least one regard, though, Rockefeller *did* cross an ethical line. After Standard had grown so large that it accounted for a significant fraction of the rail business between its Cleveland refineries and Eastern port cities in the early 1870s, Rockefeller offered to assist some railroad companies in a freight rate-fixing scheme.[10] It didn't work very well or for long, but it does highlight the lesson that companies *do* attempt to restrict competition from time to time. We have to pay careful attention to such behavior—and the antitrust authorities charged with enforcing laws against such behavior do exactly that.

For an overall judgment on Standard's conduct, though, the best thing to look at is the firm's profound and favorable effect on kerosene prices. While Rockefeller's former *rivals* may have hated him,[11] his *customers* didn't. They benefited from ever-lower prices—even as his market share grew. So, although he was eventually judged to have illegally acquired a monopoly and required to break up Standard into several smaller pieces, there's no evidence he used that market position to raise prices above

---

9 The practice of incorporating different stages of production that were previously outsourced into the normal operations of a firm is formally known as vertical integration.

10 At the time, there were several railroads competing for traffic on these routes, and they'd periodically try to form a cartel and raise rates—but one or more would inevitably cheat on the others and drive rates back to competitive levels. Rockefeller offered to punish cheaters by monitoring rail traffic and moving his oil shipments around to prevent any railroad from getting more than its agreed-upon share of the business, a role economists refer to as that of a "cartel ringmaster" coordinating the activities of the cartel's members. In exchange, Rockefeller would get some of the railroad cartel's profits.

11 As to their accusations that he had forced them from the market by setting prices below costs, the best research is by antitrust economist John McGee, who examined the record closely and concluded, "I cannot find a single instance in which Standard used predatory price cutting to force a rival refiner to sell out, to reduce asset values for purchase, or to drive a competitor out of business." See McGee, John S. "Predatory Price Cutting: The Standard Oil (N.J.) Case," *Journal of Law and Economics*, vol. 1, no. 1 (October 1958), p. 157.

competitive levels and harm consumers.[12] Unpopular as he was, Rock-efeller's genius for finding efficient and creative ways of cheaply supply-ing goods that people needed made the world a better place. A lot like Wal-Mart today.

Standard Oil may represent the first major illegal monopolization case, but it is far from the last. Microsoft and Google have been the sub-ject of antitrust cases just like Rockefeller was all those years ago. In the late 1990s, Microsoft held a dominate position in the market for computer operating systems. The Justice Department claimed that behavior such as bundling Internet Explorer and Windows into one product prevented competition and was harmful for the consumer. Predictably, Microsoft argued that this actually benefited the consumer.[13] Despite having a large market share, Microsoft now faces increasingly credible threats from more innovative alternatives such as Apple, Linux, and various mobile device operating systems.

Our indispensable second brain, Google, has also received attention from the Justice Department. There are concerns that Google can unfairly direct Internet traffic to products that it favors via its algorithms for deter-mining Web site rankings and allocating ad space. The rapidly evolving way in which entrepreneurs provide and we consume Internet content suggests, however, that Google can only take content manipulation so far before people will switch to an alternative company or technology. Though Google retains a commanding market position, there are many potential competitors waiting for signs of weakness from its products, from search engines to e-mail and maps—just as Wal-Mart faces potential competition from Costco and the Internet.

Cheaper, Faster, Better, Bigger

To understand how Wal-Mart grew from a single store in Rogers, Ar-kansas, in 1962 to become the world's largest corporation just 45 years later, it will be useful to think about the exact service it provides. Retail-ers have one basic function: Get the right products from factories and warehouses into stores so people can conveniently buy them—ideally at attractive prices.

The first step in this process is to find out what people actually want. Santa reads our wish lists, but Wal-Mart just watches what's moving out its doors, using a sophisticated inventory-management system that

---

12 That said, John McGee's frequently cited 1958 paper on Standard Oil's predatory pricing is not without critics. See Dalton, James A., and Esposito, Louis. "Predatory Price Cutting and Standard Oil: A Re-examination of the Trial Record." *Research in Law and Economics: A Journal of Policy*, vol. 22. (2007), pp. 155–205.

13 For a more detailed discussion of Microsoft's antitrust case see Fisher, Franklin, Schmalensee, Richard L., Evans, Daniel S., and Rubinfeld, Daniel L. *Did Microsoft Harm Consumers? Two Opposing Views*. Washington, DC: American Enterprise Institute, 2000.

provides information about what people are actually buying. Nowadays, though, that's true of most large retailers. What has set Wal-Mart apart?

Like Standard Oil, two key forces have made Wal-Mart successful: scale economies and technological innovation. In its early days, Wal-Mart grew faster than its rivals because of an amazingly simple policy begun by founder Sam Walton. Cheap by nature, Walton always bargained for better deals from his suppliers. At the time, though, a retailer who negotiated a discount from a wholesaler tended to leave his prices unchanged and bank higher profits. Walton passed the savings to his customers and steadily increased his sales volume—which made it easier to win further discounts from suppliers eager for his business.[14] The company's higher volume meant its overhead costs were spread over many more units sold, giving it a cost advantage over rivals.

To make this advantage clear, imagine you're going on a road trip next weekend. Before the trip you estimate that gas will cost about $100. If one of your roommates agrees to come along, the gas will cost $50 each; if all three join in, it'll only be $25 per person. Now imagine what it must be like for Wal-Mart, which sells hundreds of thousands of different products to seven billion people a year.[15] That's one hell of a road trip! At that size, Wal-Mart's success reinforces itself, because the more they sell the more they can afford to cut prices. Consider spending, say, $1 million on software that will help manage inventory better. If the company has to recover that investment from just a million customers, it would have to pass on a full dollar of these costs to each. But with seven *billion* customers a year, that works out to just 1/70th of a cent per customer.

From its very beginning, Wal-Mart was a pioneer in the application of technology to retailing. In the early 1970s, they had a basic computer network that linked individual stores with company headquarters and various distribution centers. In the 1980s, they were quick to use a revolutionary new cost-saving technology that we now take for granted—barcodes.[16] In 1987, Wal-Mart completed the largest private satellite communications network in the world.[17] Today, with 7,899 stores, two million employees, and more than 60,000 suppliers,[18] state-of-the-art communication is critical. At some point, firms can get so big that they become difficult to manage and wasteful (that is, can fall victim to scale *dis*economies).

---

14 See Frank, T.A. "Everyday Low Vices: How Much Should We Hate Wal-Mart?" *Washington Monthly*, April 2006. Available at www.washingtonmonthly.com/features/2006/0604 .frank.html.

15 Fishman, p. 6.

16 Wal-Mart. "History Timeline." Available at http://walmartstores.com/AboutUs/7603.aspx.

17 Basker, Emek, "The Causes and Consequences of Wal-Mart's Growth." *Journal of Economic Perspectives*, vol. 21, no. 3 (Summer 2007), pp. 177–198.

18 Wal-Mart. "Company Data Sheet." Available at http://walmartstores.com/FactsNews/ NewsRoom/9083.aspx.

This is another area in which Wal-Mart has been an innovator. If your company is chosen as a Wal-Mart supplier, they will actually provide you with their detailed sales data so that you know exactly how much demand there is for your product. You can then use that information to decide how much must be made and when, so you can avoid wasting money by overproducing or losing profit opportunities by underproducing.

Of course, if you fail to meet Wal-Mart's exacting standards (for price, quality, and reliability), they'll take their business elsewhere. But Wal-Mart's relationship with its suppliers is often misunderstood. The company doesn't make its suppliers jump through hoops for its own wicked pleasure. The real force that Wal-Mart's suppliers have to contend with is the consumer. Sorry, there's no dark conspiracy. Though Hollywood might have you believe otherwise, businesses and corporations don't really control people—we control them. We reward the ones that make the stuff we like with profits, and we punish the ones who don't with losses. Corporations are the puppets, consumers are the puppeteers, and profits are the strings connecting the two. For the most part, Wal-Mart provides what we want very well. It's a large, efficient, albeit controversial player in a complex worldwide system that connects suppliers to demanders. Ultimately, the most powerful members of that system are the ones with the cash: you and me.

RISKY BUSINESS

Wal-Mart has served its customers well, but—like Standard Oil, Microsoft, and Google—that doesn't mean it's a perfect organization. Some ethical lines have been crossed that can be just as important to consumers as low prices. The most widely publicized of these is Wal-Mart's mistreatment of some of its own employees. It should be noted that Wal-Mart is the largest private-sector employers in the world, with over two million people directly involved in its management, retail, and distribution network.

This immense size can at least partially explain why Wal-Mart faces so many highly publicized lawsuits each year. But they also reflect Wal-Mart's history and culture. As I mentioned before, Wal-Mart founder Sam Walton was a legendary cheapskate. Even after he became a billionaire, he kept going to his local barber shop for a $5 haircut and never left a tip![19] But he also established strong bonds with his employees and set up a profit-sharing plan that made many of them rich. After Walton died in 1992, however, his successors seemed to stress the cheap part and forget the rest of the founder's formula for good employee relations. Workers often complained that they were forced to work overtime or through lunch without pay. Wal-Mart eventually settled their lawsuits by

---

19 Frank.

agreeing to pay over $350 million to the workers and their lawyers.[20] They have since set up in-store equipment that cannot be used when employees are off the clock and have taken disciplinary actions against managers to prevent the situation from happening again.

Other critics, such as journalist David Cay Johnston, argue that when Wal-Mart enters a new community it sometimes seeks out and receives sales tax benefits from local governments.[21] A subsidy such as this could give Wal-Mart an additional edge over competitors that pay higher taxes. On the other hand, small-business owners can also use the political process to create barriers to entry for large cost-cutting retailers looking to set up shop in their communities.[22] For example, laws that establish square footage limits or various zoning restrictions intended to "preserve the aesthetic character of the community" often prevent the intrusion of chain stores and franchises.

More recently, six female employees alleged that Wal-Mart has discriminated against women, paying them less and promoting them less frequently. In a 5 to 4 opinion, the Supreme Court dismissed the case, but if Wal-Mart had lost, the results of the class-action lawsuit could have applied to well over a million employees and led to billions of dollars in damage awards (or settlement costs). That would have made it the largest job discrimination judgment in the country's history.

Clearly, for Wal-Mart (or any other company) to maintain the devotion of its customers and workers, it has to scrupulously avoid unethical behavior. Maybe not everyone does so, but most people I know avoid dealing with businesses they don't admire or trust to do the right thing. Sometimes, though, it can be hard to identify which criticisms of Wal-Mart's business practices are factual and which ones are exaggerated or misrepresented. Competitors, unions seeking to organize workers, or litigants can be just as self-interested as the big companies they're accusing of misbehavior; if we're not careful about sifting through the evidence (as many were not in evaluating claims about Standard Oil's predatory pricing), we might find ourselves simply labeling all successful corporations as evil.

OVERLOOKED BENEFITS

In sum, while there are reasons why Wal-Mart's public image is tarnished, we shouldn't just look at one side of the ledger when we make a judgment about the overall value of a firm. It's true that a company's

---

20 Greenhouse, Steven. "Wal-Mart Settles 63 Lawsuits Over Wages." *New York Times*, December 2008. Available at www.nytimes.com/2008/12/24/business/24walmart.html.

21 Although I do not agree with everything Mr. Johnston has to say about Wal-Mart's effects, you should examine his arguments for yourself. He makes some interesting points about how large retailers seek out government subsidies in *Free Lunch: How the Wealthiest Americans Enrich Themselves at Government Expense (and Stick You with the Bill)*. London: Penguin, 2007.

22 Check out Chapter 4 of this book for a more in-depth discussion of life in the political marketplace.

decisions can result in indirect costs for innocent bystanders (remember the Smiths, Joneses, and Browns back in Pleasantville), but we shouldn't ignore the direct and indirect benefits that companies like Wal-Mart contribute to our society. In competitive markets, like retailing, consumers reward the most efficient and innovative firms with profits, and those profits are a signal to other firms to do things better. As a result, you don't just get lower prices when you go to Wal-Mart. Because its rivals have adopted many of its cost-cutting technologies and business practices just to stay in the game, you also enjoy savings when you shop somewhere else. Consider this finding from economist Kenneth Rogoff:

> [T]ogether with a few sister "big box" stores (Target, Best Buy, and Home Depot), Wal-Mart accounts for roughly 50% of America's much vaunted productivity growth edge over Europe during the last decade. Fifty percent! Similar advances in wholesaling supply chains account for another 25%!…The US productivity miracle and the emergence of Wal-Mart-style retailing are virtually synonymous.[23]

On the employment front, the fact that Wal-Mart is the largest private-sector employer in the world is just part of the picture. Since, as a retailer, Wal-Mart doesn't actually manufacture the things it sells, it's estimated that an additional three million people are indirectly employed by Wal-Mart as part of its network of suppliers.[24] That means Wal-Mart is directly or indirectly responsible for the employment of over five million; only the United States government can rival that figure.

What's more, Wal-Mart's ability to connect suppliers with demanders has gotten a lot of people involved in the global economy, people who may have otherwise been left out and left much poorer. Wal-Mart has been a driving force behind globalization, a phenomenon that is raising living standards for many poor in the developing world.[25] According to one study, Wal-Mart is responsible for over 15 percent of U.S. imports of consumer products from China.[26] If Wal-Mart were a country, it would be China's eighth largest trading partner![27]

---

23 Rogoff, Kenneth. "Wall-to-Wall Wal-Mart?" Project Syndicate. May 5, 2006. Available at www.project-syndicate.org/commentary/rogoff15/English.

24 Fishman, p. 7.

25 Some of Wal-Mart's critics have accused it of "wage suppression" in developing countries, but this is simply wrong: You don't "suppress" wages by increasing the demand for labor in poor countries; you raise wages. For more on this and related issues, check out Chapter 10, "Stairway to . . . Sweat Shops?"

26 Basker, Emek, and Pham, Van H. "Wal-Mart as a Catalyst to U.S.-China Trade." University of Missouri, Dept. of Economics, Working Paper 0110, 2007.

27 Shambaugh, David. "China and the U.S.: A Marriage of Convenience." *International Herald Tribune.* January 6, 2009. Available at www.brookings.edu/opinions/2009/0106_china_shambaugh.aspx.

But the main benefit Wal-Mart contributes is the amount it saves its seven billion customers. The groceries it sells are about 15 to 25 percent cheaper, on average, than those of competing supermarkets. One 2005 study found that people who shop Wal-Mart's grocery section save 20.2 percent on food, and—an indirect benefit to non-Wal-Mart shoppers— prices at nearby groceries are 4.8 percent lower thanks to greater competition.[28] Price differences like that will have a favorable impact on the budgets of families of any income. By one estimate, these price differences save American consumers about $50 billion a year on food alone, and their savings on all of Wal-Mart's 120,000 products might be five times that much.[29] When those saved dollars are spent elsewhere, they will fuel demand and employment growth in entirely separate industries. The money might go into a college or retirement fund or make it possible for someone to afford the payment on a car and get a better job—or it just might go into savings accounts that some bank will use to make a loan to an up-and-coming small business.

Finally, it's important to note that Wal-Mart delivers its savings to those who need them most. The poor spend proportionately more of their incomes on food, and Wal-Mart customers tend to have lower incomes than many of their competitors: One survey found that the average Wal-Mart shopper earns $35,000 a year, versus $50,000 at Target and $74,000 at Costco.[30]

So, unlike Santa, Wal-Mart isn't perfect. But here's an enterprise that generates large benefits that are of special importance to those of low and modest incomes. A lot of people might consider that to be, well, progressive. We might hope that they'll do this job better, but few of us should hope they'll stop doing it entirely.

READ ON/JOIN UP

➤ For an entertaining look at the people who created some of America's most successful businesses since the 1600s—Henry Ford, Walt Disney, Ray Kroc (of McDonalds fame), Steve Jobs, you name it—see:
   Schweikart, Larry, and Pierson Doti, Lynne. *American Entrepreneur: The Fascinating Stories of the People Who Defined Business in the United States*. New York: AMACOM, 2010.

---

28 See Hausman, Jerry, and Leibtag, Ephraim. "Consumer Benefits from Increased Competition in Shopping Outlets: Measuring the Effect of Wal-Mart." MIT and Economic Research Service, U.S. Department of Agriculture, October 2005. Available at www.cemmap.ac.uk/ wps/cwp0606.pdf.

29 See: Mallaby, Sebastian. "Progressive Wal-Mart. Really." *Washington Post*. November 28, 2005. Available at www.washingtonpost.com/wp-dyn/content/article/2005/11/27/ AR2005112700687.html.

30 Ibid.

> For more on how Wal-Mart became what it is today and how it affects consumers, suppliers, employees, and competitors, see:
>> Fishman, Charles. *The Wal-Mart Effect*. London: Penguin, 2006.

> Although I do not agree with everything Mr. Johnston has to say about Wal-Mart's effect on employment, you may be interested in carefully examining his arguments for yourself. He makes some interesting points about how large retailers seek out subsidies from local governments. See:
>> Johnston, David Cay. *Free Lunch: How the Wealthiest Americans Enrich Themselves at Government Expense (and Stick you with the Bill)*.London: Penguin, 2007.

> Having studied Wal-Mart extensively, Emek Basker sheds light on the question, "Does Wal-Mart make or take jobs?" See:
>> Basker, Emek. "Job Creation or Destruction? Labor Market Effects of Wal-Mart Expansion," *Review of Economics and Statistics*, vol. 87, no. 1 (February 2005), pp. 174–183.

> Desperate to get all the facts about the story surrounding Standard Oil's predatory pricing behavior? Take a look at both of these papers to get a complete picture:
>> McGee, John S. "Predatory Price Cutting: The Standard Oil (N.J.) Case." *Journal of Law and Economics*, vol. 1, no. 1 (October 1958), pp. 137–169.
>>
>> Dalton, James A., and Esposito, Louis. "Predatory Price Cutting and Standard Oil: A Re-examination of the Trial Record." *Research in Law and Economics: A Journal of Policy*, vol. 22. (2007), pp. 155–205.

> For quick links to the Web sites discussed below, please visit *www. pearsonhighered.com/walters*:
>> For a complete list of everything Wal-Mart is accused of doing wrong, visit Walmart Watch. *Caveat emptor*: The site is funded by the Service Employees International Union, and its agenda is to bring Wal-Mart's workers into their fold.
>>
>> For useful stories, tips, and advice from real entrepreneurs in the tech industry, visit Tech Crunch.

Questions for Discussion

1. The pursuit of profit, and the amount of profit a firm earns, can be a matter of great controversy. Do some research to determine how accountants and economists differ in their definition of *profit*. Then consider how the "opportunity cost of capital" that is invested in a business should be treated in discussions about whether a company's profits are "excessive." Suppose, for example, that last year Company X's total revenue was $10 billion, and its expenses for labor, raw materials, rent, advertising, and all other items for which it had bills

and receipts totaled $9 billion, so that its reported (accounting) profit was $1 billion. Would you consider this profit rate "excessive"? Why or why not? What else might you want to know about Company X in considering this issue?

2. Suppose you are considering "predatory pricing" as a business strategy: You'll cut your prices below your costs for a while to drive your rival(s) into bankruptcy, and then you'll raises prices high enough to recover the losses you suffered once there are no more pesky competitors around. What conditions have to be satisfied for this to work? What possible problems (apart from a possible antitrust lawsuit) might make this plan fail?

3. Entrepreneurs are constantly exploring better ways to provide the things we want to buy. Some of their products and methods are accepted immediately, while others arouse major controversy. Consider the economic impact of each of the following rivalries or "transitions," and analyze why some are controversial and some are not: (a) Starbucks vs. local coffee shops; (b) personal computers vs. typewriters; (c) McDonald's vs. local burger joints; (d) CDs vs. cassettes; (e) Netflix vs. Blockbuster; (f) Amazon vs. "bricks and mortar" bookstores.

4. Many companies (including Wal-Mart) apparently enjoy major "economies of scale," which refers to the fact that their costs per unit sold have fallen as they've gotten bigger (their scale increased) and sold more output. What are some possible sources of economies of scale? Can you think of reasons why, at some scale, a firm might experience *dis*economies and see its costs per unit sold rise as it gets larger? Explain.

5. Retailers are essentially middlemen, connecting suppliers with demanders. Imagine doing the same thing yourself—buying and selling a (legal!) product on campus or in your neighborhood. Discuss the following: (a) What determines your product selection? (b) How will you determine your price(s)? (c) Where will you sell? (d) Is there an ideal size for your operation? (e) How will you manage your inventory? (f) Will you hire help? How much will you pay them? (g) Who will supply the capital you need to start the business? (h) What issues will you have to face to win customers? (i) Are there any legal barriers to starting this business?

CHAPTER 9

Spiking the Punch

Financial Markets, Principals, Agents, and Moral Hazard

by Steven A. Maex

Picture a senior prom and you got the chaperone pouring liquor into the punch bowl. Then you got the prom goers acting rude because they're all drunk. Who are you going to blame? Are you going to blame teenagers for acting crazy when they get drunk or are you going to blame the guy who spiked the punch bowl?

—PETER SCHIFF, PRESIDENT OF EURO PACIFIC CAPITAL,
DISCUSSING THE FINANCIAL CRISIS OF 2008–2009[1]

Chapter Highlights

- Financial Markets
- Interest Rates and Risk
- Principal-Agent Problems
- Incentives
- Moral Hazard

When I was 10, my family vacationed at my favorite place in the world: Colonial Williamsburg, Virginia. Now, you history buffs may be thinking that I was incredibly mature for my age; the rest may be saying, "What a nerdy little kid." In truth, I just liked Busch Gardens, the massive theme park outside town run by Anheuser-Busch, Inc. I much preferred roller coasters to 18th-century architecture and candle-making demonstrations.

Oh, I *was* intellectually inspired on that trip—though not about colonial history but about business. On a tour of the Anheuser-Busch brewery located near the park, I was amazed at the size of the factory. I'd never seen an operation of such magnitude and complexity, and I wondered how it grew to be so large. At the time, I just concluded that Mr. Busch

---

1 "Peter Schiff Analogies." Available at www.youtube.com/watch?v=vweLBpE4mso. Peter Schiff, CEO & Chief Global Strategist of Euro Pacific Capital, Inc.

must have been a very smart and rich man to get it all up and running. Though I wasn't impressed quite enough to listen very closely to the tour guide's lecture on the topic, since the "Loch Ness Monster," my first roller coaster, was calling my name.

If I *had* paid attention, I would've learned that this global enterprise was started by a man named George Schneider in 1852 when he opened the Bavarian Brewery in St. Louis, Missouri.[2] Eberhard Anheuser bought the company in 1860, and his son-in-law, Adolphus Busch, joined the venture 4 years later; the new owners renamed it the Anheuser-Busch Brewing Association in 1879. By 1901, annual production exceeded a million barrels of beer. Output reached 10 million barrels by 1964 and then 100 million by 1997. So it took twice as long to move from 1 million to 10 million barrels as it did to move from 10 million to 100 million. Why? The Prohibition era of the 1920s and 1930s certainly slowed growth, and advances in technology from the 1970s to 1997s most likely speed it up, but other factors must have also contributed to this pattern of expansion.

In 1980, something important changed at Anheuser-Busch. Up to that point, the firm was "closely held," and ownership was limited to a small group of individuals. If you wanted to buy in, you had to deal with one of these individuals directly to buy his or her stock, since it was not traded openly on an exchange.[3] This form of ownership limited the company's access to cash to finance operations and possible expansion, because only a small group of individuals had an opportunity to invest in the growth of the company. But by the late 1970s, Anheuser-Busch wanted to expand globally and needed more financial capital to do so, so it opened its doors to a much broader group of investors, listing its stock on the New York Stock Exchange (NYSE) in 1980.[4] How did this help Anheuser-Busch expand from a national to an international brewer producing more than 100 million barrels of beer annually (and building my favorite theme parks)?

To find out, we need to travel from Williamsburg to Wall Street. First we will take a look at the way financial markets enable resources to be channeled into ventures that might produce the most value for society. Then we will try to uncover some of the forces that often prevent them from achieving that laudable end.

---

2 "Anheuser-Busch – History." Available at www.anheuser-busch.com/History.html.

3 Having ownership "closely held" has its advantages. By concentrating ownership in the hands of few people, those individuals will focus their attention on the success of the enterprise. This focus diminishes as the ownership becomes more dispersed, exacerbating what is called the "principal-agent problem," which I discuss later.

4 Fun fact: If you had invested $1,000 in Anheuser-Busch stock when it was first offered to the public in 1980, it would have been worth $57,041 by 2008 (when the company was combined with the Belgian brewer InBev to become Anheuser-Busch InBev). And that's without considering the annual dividends the company paid its stockholders. *Note to self: Save money, find good growth stocks, invest.*

THE WONDERS OF WALL STREET

Let's say I want to start a new business. I find Bud Light a little bland, so I plan to create a beer company to compete with the likes of Anheuser-Busch. We'll call it Better-than-Busch Brewery (3B). But I have a problem: I'm poor. Where am I going to get the money I need to buy the factory and the equipment to launch 3B?

I have two options. First, I can borrow the money. I could go to my personal lenders, like Mom and Dad, or a bank, to obtain a loan. But they'll want me to pay interest on it, and the more doubtful they are about the brilliance of my ideas, the higher the interest rate they'll charge me. Understandable. When lenders give money to finance 3B, they're taking a risk that I might fail and won't be able to pay them back. Higher interest payments, spread out among many similarly risky borrowers, give the lender some protection against that possibility. Even if some fail, those that flourish will be able to cover any lost funds through high interest payments. And, to be honest, the risk that 3B will go bust is substantial. According to a recent study,[5] over 70 percent of start-ups fail within the first 10 years of operations. With that kind of low batting average, maybe my local bank, or even Mom and Dad, won't give me a loan at all—even at an astronomical interest rate.[6]

Thankfully, I have another option: people looking to invest in up-and-coming businesses in the hope that the success of the company will lead to riches for themselves. Sometimes, they're called venture capitalists. What's the catch? Since these investors are taking such big risks, they don't want just a fixed interest payment. They want a share of the profits if the company succeeds. Profit-sharing is often done by forming a corporation that issues stock certificates. Each certificate (or share) sold entitles the buyer to an ownership stake, the size of which is determined by the number of shares sold. The selling corporation raises cash by selling the certificates, and each buyer shares in the company's success—or failure.[7]

Sounds like a good fit for Better-than-Busch, and I'm so ambitious that I want to reach as many investors as possible by listing my company on the NYSE. I announce that 3B will have an initial public offering (IPO),

---

5 Shane, Scott A. *The Illusions of Entrepreneurship: The Costly Myths that Entrepreneurs, Investors, and Policy Makers Live By.* New Haven, CT: Yale University Press, 2008.

6 Also, regulations known as "usury laws" often prevent companies from charging interest rates that exceed some specified level, so high-risk borrowers are often shut out of loanable funds markets—unless they go to "loan sharks" who make illegal loans at high rates of interest. See "State Interest Rates and Usury Limits." *The 'Lectric Law Library.* November 13, 2010. Available at www.lectlaw.com/files/ban02.htm.

7 Obviously, investors are hoping for returns like those illustrated in footnote 4. But they can lose their entire investment if the company doesn't know what it's doing. Note also that a similar scenario can also play out under a form of ownership known as a partnership. While there is nothing called a stock certificate in a partnership, ownership interests can be sold in percentage terms to any of a number of partners.

which is the first time anyone can buy a share of my stock on the NYSE.[8] Then investors will begin to give me the cash I need in exchange for a share of ownership and a right to share in my profits. 3B is now "publicly traded," and anyone who thinks my company is worthwhile can easily become a shareholder. In principle, then, this process channels resources to the firms that investors believe might produce the most profit, which correlates with how well these firms are satisfying the needs of their customers or clients.

That said, investors are not all-seeing, all-knowing beings. Due to problems of "asymmetric information,"[9] they are sometimes unable to identify a potential problem or risk of which those *inside* the company in which they are investing may be aware. As a result, investors might mistakenly supply capital to companies that don't deserve it. This is just the first example of a theme that runs throughout this chapter: Information asymmetries and some unwholesome incentives can result in the breakdown of the desirable and efficient capital-allocation process outlined earlier. Before jumping further into this topic, though, let's consider what happens in capital markets after a company's IPO.

THE SECONDARY MARKET

While it's easy to see how an IPO that raises funds so a company can start up or expand might be beneficial to society, such initial purchases of stock are only a very small percentage of what occurs on Wall Street. If you've ever seen a stock exchange in action, it seems incredibly chaotic, with numerous traders buying and selling shares with wild motions and lots of yelling. Almost all of these transactions occur in what's called a "secondary market," where investors trade shares issued in the past. For example, after the IPO of 3B shares, anyone who wants to become an owner must purchase preowned shares in this portion of the market. That doesn't raise any new funds for the company, as did the initial IPO, but only changes the ownership of the existing shares. What are *those* trades good for?

First, of course, if you couldn't conveniently resell ownership shares in 3B, would you buy it in the first place? Maybe—but you'd probably pay less for such shares, so the secondary market supports (and is inseparable from) my IPO.

---

8 Actually, the most common way for a company to execute an IPO is to have an investment bank underwrite the offering. In this situation, the bank will purchase all of the released stock up front and then be responsible for selling it to interested parties.

9 *Asymmetric information* is a fancy term for cases in which one party in a transaction has more information than the other(s). As a result, those possessing this additional information are in position to make better decisions regarding that particular transaction, which increases their chances of gaining the upper hand over their counterparts within the exchange and capitalizing on it.

What's more, having 3B stock trade publicly and frequently will help me run my company better, even if trades of those initial shares don't bring me any more cash. When investors put their wealth on the line, they have a pretty strong incentive to figure out (using objective information) which companies are being run well or badly. The rise and fall of stock prices can therefore send some important signals and affect who gets capital and who doesn't.

Suppose, for example, that 3B makes an ale that consumers can't get enough of, and profits are high. Great! Since consumers want more of my ale than I can supply, I need to brew more. I can do that by putting my profits back into the company (retaining my earnings) and building more breweries, but the stock market gives me another, maybe quicker, financing option. My high profits and rising stock price might enable me to issue more shares, bring in more money, and expand operations. If, on the other hand, my ale is unpopular, investors might start to dump their stock and 3B's price would go down, sending me a message that I need to make better decisions. It would also make it harder for me to raise cash by selling additional shares. From a social and individual standpoint, then, it's all good: Financial capital is scarce, and we want it to go where the payoff is greatest. When shares are publicly traded, the goal of the individual investor and the economy at large are aligned, with capital flowing to firms that are doing a good job of satisfying consumers and away from those that aren't.

However, it's not only corporations that gain from these markets. Investors also benefit from the ability to invest small amounts of money in many *different* companies. As I mentioned before, starting a new business is a risky proposition, and even well-established products can become unpopular or obsolete, like America Online or Blockbuster, to name two. Investors can never be sure which ones will or will not succeed. They can reduce their risk by not putting all their eggs in one basket or, in investment jargon, diversifying their portfolios. If you have a diverse portfolio and one company in it performs badly or fails, all of your wealth isn't destroyed. If people couldn't diversify, they wouldn't want to put as much wealth at risk and would inevitably invest much less. As a result, companies wouldn't have access to nearly as much capital to finance research and development or expansion, and society may not be privileged to have the resulting products at its disposal. And we'd all be poorer.

Finally, trades in the secondary market can *discipline* the managers of a company. If a "fat cat" CEO implements bad strategies or tolerates inefficiency within a company, discouraged investors sell its stock. If its price falls low enough, though, some savvy investors might buy enough shares to take control of the company and fire the incompetent managers in the hopes of benefiting from a higher stock price once the company gets back on track.

PAPER PUSHERS

If you've seen Oliver Stone's 1987 classic *Wall Street* (or the 2010 sequel), you know the negative light in which financiers are portrayed in the mainstream media. The film centers on Bud Fox (played by Charlie Sheen), a young Wall Street trader, and his quest to follow in the footsteps of corporate raider Gordon Gekko (Michael Douglas). One of the film's themes is the contrast between the greed-driven Gekko[10] and the selfless, admirable Carl Fox (Martin Sheen), Bud's father. It's Carl's advice to Bud that sums up the attitude many Americans have toward Wall Street and those who make their living there: "Stop going for the easy buck and start producing something with your life. Create, instead of living off the buying and selling of others."[11]

On the surface, at least, Carl Fox has a point. Wall Street stock and bond dealers don't make anything tangible that others can use. They don't build cars or houses or even cook meals at the local steakhouse. All they do is trade little pieces of paper in the hope of making a profit. What value could that possibly provide for society?

But remember: If we want the makers of good products to expand (and the makers of bad ones not to), Wall Street has to operate efficiently and provide worthy companies with the capital they need. *That's* the "good" that traders produce. They may not even think of it that way; they're just trying to buy low, sell high, and bank profits. But they can't make much of a living doing that unless they're good at identifying companies that are likely to grow and prosper (i.e., the ones making what we want, at prices we like).[12] To make a profit, they'll be highly motivated to gather lots of information about what companies are doing and become very skilled at analyzing those companies' strategies. Then, as thousands of traders buy and sell shares based on their knowledge—or advise others to do so—they'll move stock prices in ways that channel more or less resources to these companies.

In addition, traders are "disciplinarians." Many companies base a lot of their executives' compensation on their stock's price. When traders decide that a company isn't performing to its potential and start selling shares, resulting in a falling stock price, the traders can effectively punish that company's executives for inefficient behavior. In the extreme, when the executives don't get the message the market is sending, a raider like Gekko might come along, buy enough shares to take control of the firm and fire those

---

10 Stone evidently thought that naming this character after a lizard would leave no doubt about who the bad guy was. A generation later, though, a cute little gecko is a popular spokesman for a major insurance company.

11 *Wall Street*. Dir. Oliver Stone. 20th Century Fox Film Corporation, 1987.

12 Alternatively, identifying companies that are headed downhill can be useful, too: Traders can take a financial position ("sell short") that will enable them to profit if the company's stock price falls, and in the process they send signals that the company can do better.

executives, and put it on a more profitable, socially useful course. Which is, despite what Carl Fox might think, "producing something."

"WALL STREET GOT DRUNK"

Unfortunately, though, as mentioned earlier, our financial markets don't always work as well in practice as they do in theory. We don't need to look any further than the financial crisis that began in 2007 (and whose effects are still being felt as this is written) to see how Wall Street can spin out of control. On October 9, 2007, the Dow Jones Industrial Average closed at its highest point in history at 14,164.53; just 17 months later, it had fallen by over 50 percent. If your retirement nest egg was invested in the stocks making up the Dow index and was worth $250,000 on October 9, 2007, you had less than $115,000 by March 6, 2009.

As the meltdown proceeded, Americans made a long list of people to blame: corrupt traders,[13] short sellers,[14] greedy investment bankers, and incompetent or inadequately armed regulators (depending on your point of view). President George W. Bush's assessment of the situation was summarized in the now-famous line that "Wall Street got drunk."[15]

Why would rational individuals act like drunks? Entire books have been and will be written about this period of economic history; we don't have space to do justice to all the sophisticated explanations of this world-wide financial crisis in this chapter. We can, however, shed light on three key economic concepts that are at the heart of a lot of those explanations: *the principal-agent problem*, *adverse selection*, and *moral hazard*.

IT'S NOT THAT I'M LAZY...

The 1999 film *Office Space* was a hilarious take on corporate America at the height of the "dot-com boom." In it, Peter Gibbons (played by Ron Livingston) was a disgruntled employee whose mind had been numbed by his boring office job. When consultants were brought in to increase company efficiency and asked Peter about his poor work ethic, Peter's explanation was simple: "It's not that I'm lazy. It's that I just don't care . . . . It's a problem of motivation, all right? Now if I work my

---

13 Such as Bernie Madoff, who is now serving a 150-year sentence for defrauding those who invested in what turned out to be a pyramid scheme.

14 Short selling is the practice of borrowing securities (stocks, bonds, etc.) and selling them in the hopes that the price will fall. When (if) it does, the short seller will have made a gain since he or she will be able to repurchase the security at the lower price than it was originally sold in order to pay back the loan. Short sellers are sometimes blamed (errantly) for "bear" markets since many see them as exacerbating an already declining market by betting that it will continue to fall. Taking this view to the extreme, some countries even outlawed short selling with the goal of curbing market turmoil during the financial crisis.

15 "President Bush: 'Wall Street Got Drunk.'" *MSNBC*. Available at www.youtube.com/watch?v=bT29fq0slGc.

ass off and Initech ships a few extra units, I don't see another dime, so where's the motivation?"[16]

What Peter is describing is an example of the principal-agent problem. Think about 3B now that it has become a publicly traded firm with many owners ("principals"). These owners can't oversee the day-to-day operations of the firm, so they hire executives and managers ("agents") to represent their best interests. The principals hope that their firm will generate as much profit as possible, but their agents—especially if they're paid a salary that, like Peter's, isn't closely tied to performance—might not have much incentive to work harder than the minimum required to keep their jobs.

Of course, principals aren't stupid. To address this problem, they'll try to monitor their executives' performances as best they can—but that can be difficult (from afar) and expensive (with many agents to keep track of). To cope with these monitoring problems, they'll also try to strengthen their agents' incentives to make efficient decisions. They might compensate them with things like stock options (which have value only if the company's stock price exceeds some threshold) or profit-sharing to align the goals of management with those of owners. Ultimately, though, there's no perfect cure for the principal-agent problem—just treatments that can reduce the pain it can produce. Sometimes that pain can be low profits; sometimes it can mean excessive risk or damage to the firm's reputation.

Who Spiked the Punch?

If you've ever read the fine print on a lottery ticket, you might think lotteries are a sucker's bet. A typical $1 "pick 4" ticket, for example, gives you a 1-in-1,000 chance of winning $500, so it has an expected value of only 50 cents. This is, in fact, why lotteries make so much money for local and state governments—and why you probably should avoid them (even if you're "legal").[17]

But now suppose I change the rules a bit and set up a company that buys *used* lottery tickets for their face value. Great! If you win, the jackpot's all yours; but if your number doesn't come up, just bring your ticket to me and, in effect, get your wager back. It's a "heads you win, tails I lose" situation.

This scenario illustrates two pivotal economic concepts that were a big factor in the financial crisis. First, think of whether the company above could ever be a successful business venture. Who are the only people that

---

16 *Office Space.* 20th Century Fox Film Corporation, 1999.

17 The fact that many people do *not* avoid lotteries has provoked economists to think of reasons this behavior might not be crazy; most have to do with how the psychic value of a large if very unlikely reward might exceed a trivially small outlay. Others might just say, "There's a sucker born every minute."

would bring me their used lottery tickets? The losers, obviously. This illustrates the concept of adverse selection, which stems from asymmetrical information: The holders of tickets know whether they won or lost and whether it would benefit them to come to me for the return of its face value—but I don't.

This not only leaves me with an "adverse selection" of tickets but induces you to take more risks. In this situation, you'd be foolish not to bet aggressively since you can rest assured that you will be able to get back the amount that you paid for the ticket. This removal of risk (or, really, transfer of risk from you to me) is "moral hazard" in a nutshell. In many markets—some dealing in financial assets, some in real estate—individuals and firms were able to take positions that were insulated from downside risk. As a result, they made much bigger and riskier bets than they would without that insulation.

But wait, you might say, that seems nuts. In the real world, no one would offer to buy worthless lottery tickets for their face value. While that may be true, what *did* happen wasn't much different. Certain institutions encouraged people to make ever-more-risky investments and then pass them on to others who (a) didn't particularly care about these risks, (b) didn't understand them, or (c) were simply lied to about them. Let's briefly examine some real-world examples and how they contributed to moral hazard problems.

Freddie, Fannie, and Not-Very-Secure Securities

In the third quarter of 2006, home values—after years of rapid appreciation—started to fall, and fall hard. Though some economists had been warning for quite a while that housing prices were unrealistically high—and, in fact, that this "bubble" had to burst—their words had fallen on deaf ears.[18] Some of the fuel for this price inflation had come from financial institutions that were determined to lend to very risky ("subprime") borrowers, such as those with poor credit ratings and little savings, who then found it easy to qualify for mortgage loans that they used to bid up home prices. And when prices started to slide, it was partly because many of these high-risk borrowers couldn't make their mortgage payments, started defaulting on their loans, and put a glut of foreclosed homes on the market.

Naturally, many questioned why so many lending institutions had taken such large risks in the subprime market. The answer is that they felt insulated from these risks, while they could capture the gains from lending ever-larger amounts.

---

18 See, for example, the work of Yale economist Robert Shiller, as summarized in Leonhardt, David. "Be Warned: Mr. Bubble's Worried Again." *The New York Times.* August 21, 2005. Available at www.nytimes.com/2005/08/21/business/yourmoney/21real.html.

For example, two government-sponsored enterprises (GSEs) called Freddie Mac and Fannie Mae[19] encouraged subprime loans and willingly took on the risk when they were made. When a lender completed a loan agreement with a borrower, Freddie and Fannie would buy it at an attractive price (and also pay the loan originator a fee to service the loan). That both allowed the lender to avoid any risk that the borrower would default and supplied the lender with fresh cash—which could be loaned to someone else. Freddie and Fannie meant well—their stated goal was to broaden home ownership in the United States—but the effect of their policies was to create a strong incentive for banks to reach ever deeper into the pool of loan applicants and inevitably make some bad bets. But since Fannie and Freddie were happy to take those off their hands—like used lottery tickets—the banks had no reason to stop.[20]

Freddie and Fannie aside, Wall Street entrepreneurs figured out another way to insulate themselves from risk. Bundling a lot of small mortgage loans together, they created a new type of instrument called a mortgage-backed security (MBS), sometimes called a mortgage pass-through. Buyers of an MBS received all the interest and principal payments on the underlying mortgages, and they assumed that a diversified pool of such loans was a safe investment. As a result of this perceived safety, the MBS market took off. After all, the homes that these mortgages had been used to buy was collateral, so what could go wrong?

By now it should be obvious: If *you* make a loan and depend on the borrower to repay, you'll pick those borrowers very carefully. If you can pass those loans along to someone else in a big bundle (that, perhaps, nobody is inspecting very carefully) you'll be much less careful. If the borrowers you pick don't pay, it's somebody else's problem. Again, the incentive to make bad bets is strong.[21] In sum, these new "securities" weren't very secure: They were ticking time bombs in the portfolios of unsuspecting investors, and when mortgage default rates started to rise and home prices started to fall, the consequences were catastrophic for financial institutions, individuals, and even governments holding MBSs.

---

19 More fully, the Federal Home Mortgage Corporation and the Federal National Mortgage Association, respectively.

20 See, e.g., Woods, Thomas E. *Meltdown*. Washington, DC: Regnery Publishing, 2009. Estimates of the cost to taxpayers of all the bad loans Freddie and Fannie own sometimes range as high as $1 trillion, though more "optimistic" scenarios put the potential costs under $400 billion; it will depend on how many borrowers eventually default and how low home prices eventually go.

21 Remarkably, one investment Web site touted these new securities by pointing out that "an MBS is a way for a smaller regional bank to lend mortgages to its customers without having to worry about whether the customers have the assets to cover the loan" (see www.investopedia.com/terms/m/mbs.asp). But it's the lender's *job* to "worry about" whether the borrower will repay a loan; not doing so is a good illustration of moral hazard.

Unfortunately, there were so many bad loans on the books of so many institutions that it was hard to tell ones that had avoided excess risk and were solvent from ones that weren't. Panic set in. Federal officials at the Treasury Department and the Federal Reserve decided that to prevent credit markets from melting down entirely while things got sorted out, they had to step in and "bail out" some of the biggest players in these markets with infusions of cash. Aside from the huge costs to taxpayers, critics pointed out that this worsened moral hazard problems. If a bank is judged too big to be allowed to fail because this would destabilize financial markets and have unacceptable macroeconomic consequences, then it will have an incentive to take excessive risks since it will capture the gains if the risks pay off and taxpayers will help cover losses if not. In sum, telling financial institutions to "get big and go for broke, because taxpayers will be there to protect you when things fall apart" is a dangerous message to send.

Of course, boiling down a complex financial crisis to the key items discussed here is clearly oversimplifying the matter. Entire books have been and continue to be written on the topic, and therefore a few paragraphs cannot do it justice. However, the main purpose of this discussion is to evidence that there are real consequences of the theoretical topics and hypothetical examples of adverse selection and moral hazard outlined earlier.[22]

SOBERING UP

So where do we go from here? Given the crucial role that financial markets serve in allocating capital, they're not going away—nor should they. Perhaps even a majority of "Occupy Wall Street" protesters might agree that capital markets do such important work that they need to be improved rather than abolished.

To assist in that task, the Dodd-Frank Wall Street Reform and Consumer Protection Act, which advocates claim will prevent future crises by better addressing information asymmetry and moral hazard issues, was signed into law in July 2010. It has commonly been described as the most sweeping overhaul of the regulations affecting banks and other financial institutions since the Great Depression of the 1930s.

In its final form, the Dodd-Frank Act is 848 pages long, so it's not easy to summarize. It creates several new federal agencies and requires them to write hundreds of new rules affecting conduct in financial markets in an attempt to "promote the financial stability of the United States

---

22 For a more complete picture of the failure of the financial markets from 2007–2009, please see Woods' *Meltdown* and Lewis's *The Big Short*, which are listed in the Read On/Join Up section at the end of this chapter.

by improving accountability and transparency in the financial system, to end 'too big to fail,' to protect the American taxpayer by ending bailouts, to protect consumers from abusive financial services practices, and for other purposes."[23]

Will it work? Only time will tell, but unfortunately, regulators, like investors, are fallible beings. New rules can change how we play the game, but whether we play it better will depend, in part, on how the rules alter our incentives.

As long as there are large-scale enterprises there will be principal-agent problems—and such problems will even bedevil the government sector (where we voters and taxpayers are the principals and politicians and bureaucrats are our agents) as well as private-sector firms. And as long as we humans are involved in taking risks, some of us will look for ways to find loopholes in the rules that allow us to keep the winnings from our successful bets and to offload our losses to others. It's worth remembering that the players in the housing bubble weren't just big Wall Street investment banks. A lot of people like us borrowed heavily in hopes of scoring capital gains as home prices inflated and then walked away from these investments and left our lenders on the hook for our losses when, instead, values tanked.[24] As it turns out, whether we're talking about government policymakers, big-time financiers, or ordinary homeowners, bad incentives can lead to very bad results.

READ ON/JOIN UP

➤ For one of the most complete (and entertaining) accounts of how some Wall Streeters built the mortgage-backed securities market while others saw the dangers that it contained, see:

Lewis, Michael. *The Big Short: Inside the Doomsday Machine.* New York: W.W. Norton, 2010.

➤ For a dramatic account about how one intrepid analyst figured out how the Madoff investment empire was a fraud, warned federal regulators, and nevertheless was ignored, see:

Markopolis, Harry. *No One Would Listen: A True Financial Thriller.* Hoboken, NJ: John Wiley & Sons, 2010.

---

23 111th Congress, Dodd–Frank Wall Street Reform and Consumer Protection Act. Available at http://frwebgate.access.gpo.gov/cgi-bin/getdoc.cgi?dbname=111_cong_bills&docid=f:h4173enr.txt.pdf.

24 This tactic is now described in the press as "strategic default." It turns out that most mortgages are "non-recourse loans," meaning that if the borrower walks away, the lender can repossess the house and sell it but has no other recourse (i.e., can't force the lender to sell other assets to pay back the full amount owed). Again, "heads I win, tails you lose."

➢ For a free-market look at some of the potential causes of the financial collapse, including many of the topics mentioned within this chapter, see:

Woods, Thomas. *Meltdown: A Free-Market Look at Why the Stock Market Collapsed, the Economy Tanked, and Government Bailouts Will Make Things Worse.* Washington, DC: Regnery Publishing, 2009.

➢ For a quick link to a Web site addressing the topic below, please visit *www.pearsonhighered.com/walters*:

If you share some of my enthusiasm for business, consider getting involved with Junior Achievement. You'll find lots of ways to teach kids about the importance of entrepreneurship and economics, including financial markets.

QUESTIONS FOR DISCUSSION

1. How, exactly, does charging higher interest rates to "risky" borrowers really protect lenders? As you consider that question, it might be helpful to think about this example: Suppose you have a million dollars to lend, and there is one borrower (call him "Uncle Sam") who is willing to pay 3 percent interest on a million-dollar loan. You are absolutely certain he'll pay back every penny you lend to him. Then there are many other borrowers willing to pay 10 percent interest on smaller loans of $50,000 each—but history shows that 1 out of every 20 of these borrowers will go bankrupt and fail to pay back anything (principle or interest). Do the math: How much money will you make if you choose to lend to the risky borrowers instead of Uncle Sam? Extra credit: What's the lowest interest rate that would make you willing to lend to these risky borrowers?

2. Anheuser-Busch didn't "go public" until 1980. Why do you think it took them so long to discover the virtues of equity markets (i.e., what were the benefits the family might have seen in remaining "closely held")? Some companies that have been publicly traded for many years eventually are "taken private." Why do you think this might happen?

3. Executive compensation in U.S. companies has become an increasingly controversial topic as the pay of top executives has risen relative to that of other workers. Much of this compensation is in the form of bonuses that are tied to firms' stock prices. Some argue that such bonuses are necessary to address principal-agent problems and ensure that executives have appropriate incentives to maximize shareholders' wealth (which, clearly, depends on stock prices). Others argue that there are some perverse incentives in such compensation schemes. What problems do you see in tying executive compensation to stock prices? Does such compensation solve principal-agent problems or make them worse?

4. Moral hazard obviously played a huge role in the worldwide financial crisis with which we are still coping. But you probably have seen examples of moral hazard in other contexts, and perhaps in your own life experience. Identify such an example, describe how it fits the definition of moral hazard, and consider how potential problems arising from it might be prevented or addressed.

5. Suppose you borrowed $400,000 to buy a home at the peak of the real estate "bubble" in 2006, and today that home is only worth $200,000, or roughly half as much as you owe the bank from which you borrowed. Your brother says you should "strategically default" and walk away from this loan, even though you have a decent job and can afford to make your monthly mortgage payment. Do some research and determine what the financial benefits and costs of your brother's strategy would be. Would you feel ethically bound to pay back the loan even if you concluded that the financial benefits of default exceeded the costs?

CHAPTER 10

Stairway to...
Sweatshops?

What Foreign Factories Mean for You, Me, and the Developing World

by Daniel G. O'Neill

> *The misery of being exploited by capitalists is nothing compared to the misery of not being exploited at all.*
>
> —CAMBRIDGE UNIVERSITY ECONOMIST JOAN ROBINSON[1]

Chapter Highlights

- Market Competition
- Outsourcing
- Economic Development
- Costs and Production
- Fair Trade

I can't stand jogging. I've never enjoyed it or most of the things that go with it, like early mornings, cold weather, and treadmills. You, on the other hand, actually like jogging. You love the fresh air, the exercise, and the solitude before a busy day. In fact, you enjoy jogging so much so that you've worn out your best running shoes.

So you head to the store and consider your options. Nike, Reebok, or New Balance? Style? Color? Size? You can find the perfect shoes at your local Foot Locker or at countless other stores across the United States. If you really wanted to, you could purchase a pair of sneakers that measures your heart rate and DJs your iPod.

These options are probably available within just a few miles of where you live, and for a mere $50 or $60. You might even get a second pair for half price. Just as important, your new running shoes (no matter which

---

1 Robinson, Joan. *Economic Philosophy*. New Brunswick, NJ: Aldine Transaction Publishing, 2006, p. 45.

famous brand you select) will probably last for years. Style, quality, and impact-absorbing air-bubble technology, all for one low price.

If you look in your closet right now, I'd bet that each pair of shoes you own is unique in some way. But they all likely have one thing in common: They were made somewhere far, far away. Footwear ranging from sneakers to dress shoes, flip flops to work boots, is made in places like Nicaragua, Vietnam, and of course China. And made pretty cheap, too.

Do you ever think about the workers who make our shoes? It's crossed my mind, and I know I'm not alone. There's a big movement in America that wants to make sure that the workers who do things like sew our T-shirts, pick our coffee beans, and assemble our gadgets are treated and paid *fairly*. This concept of "fairness" is sort of a slippery one, though. It's hard to come to a consensus on what "fair" means. If my idea of fairness is different from yours, whose opinion should rule?

Most of us can agree, however, that the people who make our stuff should have roofs over their heads and food in their stomachs. We think, justifiably, that everyone should have the opportunity to earn enough money not just to survive but to enjoy a decent standard of living. We read appalling descriptions of the terrible working conditions in foreign factories. We're blown away when we hear that workers are paid only a few cents an hour for their honest hard work. And, naturally, we develop a dislike for these factories, commonly labeled "sweatshops."

Technically, the U.S. Government Accountability Office defines a sweatshop as "an employer that violates more than one federal or state labor law governing minimum wage and overtime, child labor, industrial homework, occupational safety and health, worker's compensation or industry regulation."[2] But most people use the term more broadly to describe any workplace that involves conditions they deem to be nasty and/or pays wages they consider exploitive, and that's the way I'll use the term throughout this chapter.

Before we dive into our exploration of why such factories exist and the effects they have on the global economy, let's put aside our preconceptions and try to answer the question: Why are sweatshops so bad?

How to Make Cheap Stuff

We'll start back at the Foot Locker, where you're shopping for your new running shoes. When you compare prices in the store, all you're really seeing is the final product and price tag. But what factors determine that sticker price? And, more important for this chapter, how can it possibly be so low?

---

2 United States General Accounting Office. "Garment Industry: Efforts to Address the Prevalence and Conditions of Sweatshops." November 1994. Available at www.gao.gov/archive/1995/he95029.pdf.

Competition among firms plays a big part in driving prices down. Nike and Reebok and lots of other shoe companies are constantly trying to get your business and mine (even though I don't jog). Since people are different, shoe companies offer a variety of styles at different prices. Not everyone is willing to pay for the latest and greatest sneaker technology. But each shoe company tries to strike that balance of price and quality that will get us to buy their brand instead of another. If they can do that on a regular basis, they can stay in business.

Cutting production costs while maintaining quality has been a popular business strategy since day one, and modern shoe companies are no different. Since wages are such a significant part of a company's expenses, cutting wages can be an effective way to keep overall costs low.[3]

While lower wages may be in the best interest of the firm, the employees facing pay cuts wouldn't be too happy about the prospect of reduced incomes. Historically, U.S. workers often formed labor unions to bargain collectively for higher wages or simply threatened to work elsewhere if they felt they weren't paid well enough. And in this "land of opportunity," labor demand has usually (though not in recessions!) been strong enough to make employers take those threats seriously.

The wage demands of American workers are a major roadblock for U.S. shoe companies trying to cut costs. Higher costs mean higher sticker prices at Foot Locker and fewer shoe sales. And higher wages would naturally increase the cost of making shoes, unless workers became more productive as a result of their higher wages (like Henry Ford's employees in footnote 3).

So shoe companies have looked elsewhere to lower their costs. Turning their eyes globally, they have begun to produce in countries where workers will accept lower wages without sacrificing too much productivity. And shoe companies aren't alone. From textile workers to customer service representatives to tax preparers, jobs go to those in other parts of the world willing to work for less, a phenomenon that has come to be known as international outsourcing or offshoring.

In developing countries, like much of Asia and Latin America, there are a whole lot of people willing to take these jobs for less money than most Americans are, even if that requires working in a dirty factory. In

---

3 Cost-cutting doesn't always mean wage-cutting, though. A great example is Henry Ford's five-dollar day. In the early 1900s, Ford paid his employees $2.34 per day to build Model Ts. Even though this was the going rate for factory work in Detroit, Ford's employees were not always the most productive; they'd occasionally even show up for work drunk. They knew that if they got fired, they could find a job that paid about the same somewhere else. In 1914, after Ford radically raised wages to five dollars a day, his workers began to care more about keeping their jobs, and as a result the assembly line began to move faster. Much faster. The company's profits doubled in a span of 2 years, and Ford was quoted as saying, "The payment of five dollars a day for an eight-hour day was one of the finest cost-cutting moves we ever made." Ford, Henry, and Crowther, Samuel. *My Life and Work*. Garden City, NY: Doubleday, Page & Co., 1922. For more details, see http://web.bryant.edu/~ehu/h364proj/summ_99/armoush/index.htm.

economic terms, the supply of labor is high relative to demand in these regions of the world.

By hiring workers in foreign countries, shoe companies are able to cut costs dramatically. Instead of paying U.S. wages in a nation where high labor demand has pushed up average wages, companies take advantage of the relatively low labor demand and low average wages in other countries. They set up factories in remote parts of the world and train workers to make their products. Americans (and everyone, really) have cheaper shoes, T-shirts, and iPods, among many other things, as a result.

Is this "fair" to the poor factory workers in developing countries? They spend hours a day assembling our products in the sweltering heat, and some of them get as little as 13 cents an hour.[4] Many people argue that these working conditions are unfair and inhumane because they are not the same conditions under which Americans work. A lot of us feel that these sweatshops should be shut down or at the very least that they should be forced to pay their workers more. But should they?

An "Alternative" View of Sweatshops

Maybe not. And it's not because high wages and good working conditions are inherently bad things. On the contrary, they're wonderful when they come about naturally—which they will, over time, as workers gain access to more employment options and employers begin competing for the best workers. But *forcing* higher labor costs on a factory in the developing world has two major unintended consequences: driving production out of developing countries and driving up the price of the goods produced. Before we explore these two consequences, however, let's look at the reasons why people in developing nations would choose to work in these notoriously horrible factories in the first place.

Before factories started opening their doors in poor countries, much of the population worked as subsistence farmers, and many still do. They had no other options; it was often a choice between farming and starving. These farmers worked long, grueling days and grew enough to survive and (if they were lucky) to sell or trade for a few other necessities. Because there were no viable alternatives, they did whatever was necessary to stay alive. Often, this was difficult, painful, dangerous, and tiresome. That's why, sometimes, even the low wages that factories offered were a welcome opportunity for workers to earn a better living.

At the same time, low wages were an advantage for the developing world, and they still are. They are the reason that American corporations

---

4 Average hourly apparel worker's wage in Bangladesh. Powell, Benjamin, and Skarbek, David. "Sweatshops and Third World Living Standards: Are the Jobs Worth the Sweat?" September 27, 2004. The Independent Institute. Available at www.independent.org/publications/working_papers/article.asp?id=1369.

set up factories in poor nations in the first place. Sweatshop workers might admire American pay scales, but having the opportunity to work in a factory is likely to be more important to them than how their wages compare to an American's. The fact that these men and women go to work every day is convincing evidence that the benefits of factory work (income) outweigh the costs (sweat).

This brings us to our first consequence of paying U.S. wages to workers in developing countries: driving production *out* of developing nations. Imagine that U.S. wages were deemed to be "fair" and were required to be paid across the globe. Why would a company choose to produce goods in Indonesia when the wages there are the same as those in Indiana? Assuming the product was to be sold primarily in the United States, the firm could lower its transportation costs by setting up shop in the Midwest rather than the Far East.

By mandating U.S. wages for foreign factory workers, we've effectively closed down many of the factories in Indonesia. Suddenly all those low-paying jobs in Indonesia have been eliminated.[5] We've reduced the choices that Indonesian workers have for employment, eliminating what might have even been their best option, and limited them to less attractive ones, like subsistence farming.

You may agree that paying Indiana wages in Indonesia is unrealistic, and even that such a policy would destroy a lot of jobs. But why can't we just pay sweatshop workers a little more—maybe half the current U.S. wage? We'd maintain the advantages of having a factory in Indonesia (i.e., lower wages relative to those in the United States), and Indonesian workers would be better off. What's wrong with that?

Well, a second unintended consequence of these higher wages is higher cost of production. More expensive labor means more expensive stuff. And if stuff is more expensive when we see it in the store, then we won't buy as much of it.[6] As a direct result of our making fewer purchases, factories won't produce as many goods, meaning they won't need to hire as many factory workers. Some factory workers would get a raise, but others would have to settle for their second-best option, like farming.

So, even though the factory might keep its doors open, paying wages that are even a little bit higher would leave some of the native labor force

---

5 Economists call this "input substitution." Here, Indiana workers would be substituted for Indonesian ones.

6 This is "output substitution." In place of Indonesian-made shoes, we'd buy Indiana-made ones, or other products entirely.

7 There have been many efforts to maintain "fair wages" within the United States and elsewhere. We're all familiar with minimum wage laws, and some cities and states have even higher "living wages" that are mandated by law. Living wages are intended to represent the minimum income deemed necessary for a person to live and provide basic food, shelter, and clothing. Despite their good intentions, this type of law pushes up production costs and, in turn, reduces the demand for products as well as employment.

(to say nothing of you and me) worse off. Is this fair? Are the gains of some people worth more than the losses to others? These are hard questions that economists usually don't try to answer, but the tools of economics can help point out the trade-offs.[7]

A key thing to remember is that the arrival of a factory won't reduce the quality of life of local workers. It'll just give them another option, of which they can take advantage or completely ignore. The fact that workers are willing to take factory jobs leads me to believe that such jobs are better than the workers' other alternatives.

Case in point: In Honduras, the average apparel worker earns $13.10 a day. This may sound low to the average American, but consider that 44 percent of the population of Honduras lives on less than $2 a day.[8] Honduran textile workers are actually highly paid relative to other occupations.

Of course, a common criticism of sweatshops is that workers are not *choosing* to work in them but are forced to do so, sometimes even as young children. I am strictly opposed to the use of force in obtaining workers, no matter what the circumstances. Regrettably, throughout history there have been all too many examples of forced labor and enslavement. Although this type of corruption is a serious problem, the "sweatshop" label is also regularly applied to factories where employees are freely choosing to show up to work each day. These workers are not the ones being exploited. They are simply taking advantage of the opportunity to work. Coercion involving threats or violence is a different matter altogether.

STEP RIGHT UP TO DEVELOPMENT

Sometimes factories get a bad reputation, but historically they have been an important part of the development process and have led to major improvements in quality of life. The Industrial Revolution in Great Britain and the United States, which was driven by factory labor in conditions not too different from today's sweatshops, started a gradual 150-year process of improvement that created what we now see as advanced societies. Similar advances have happened more recently in a few Pacific Rim countries, like Japan, South Korea, Hong Kong, and Taiwan. It only took these "Asian Tigers" around 30 years to develop.

Because of freer trade, including transfers of technology or ideas (the Internet comes to mind), poor countries now can develop at an even faster pace than their predecessors. Industrialization has made life so much better in so many parts of the modern world, as the graph below

---

8 Powell, Benjamin, and Skarbek, David. "Don't Get in a Lather Over Sweatshops." *Christian Science Monitor.* August 2, 2005. Available at www.csmonitor.com/2005/0802/p09s02-coop. html.

Figure 10–1 GDP per Capita

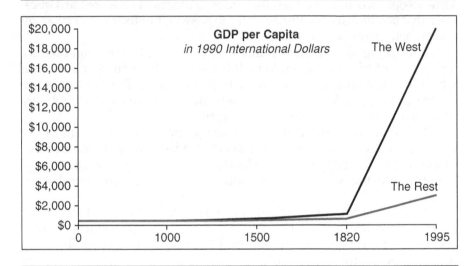

Source: Author created based on data from the article Maddison, Angus. "Poor Until 1820." Available at www2.econ.iastate.edu/classes/econ355/choi/rankh.htm. "The West" includes Western Europe, North America, and Japan; "The Rest" includes Latin America, Africa, China, "Other Europe," and "Other Asia."

shows.[9] Even in the developing world, we're seeing gains from global-ization, although there's still a lot of catching up to do. If we want to see "The Rest" catch up to "The West," we need to promote its development, not prevent it. And forcing higher wages on foreign factories is a surefire way to slow down development.

Sweatshop-type factories are part of the first steps in lifting a devel-oping nation out of a cycle of poverty and hardship. The development process has been compared to a stairway or a ladder, and the climb must begin somewhere. Calls for higher wages or better working conditions are the equivalent of trying to skip stairs. Each seems like a nice shortcut, but since they both lead to the unintended consequences of higher prices in the United States and less employment in the developing world, they're really too good to be true. Instead of helping poor countries advance, arbitrarily setting wages at higher levels would effectively knock these nations off the development staircase before they could really get started on the climb.

Former Nicaraguan foreign minister Francisco Aguirre-Sacasa had similar thoughts about attempts to shut down Nicaraguan factories. He said, "They are not trying to help our workers; by causing firms to leave

---

9 If this seems like a pointless graph, substitute "standard of living" in place of "GDP per capita," and "Industrial Revolution" in place of "1820."

they are going to leave our workers in the lurch. . . . We are on the first rung of the ladder. It is important that we are not knocked off."[10]

BUY MEXICAN

Of course, no one in America actually wants to knock poor countries off the development ladder, right? You might be surprised.

We have already seen that forcing better wages and conditions on sweatshop workers is bad for a lot of different people, including the average American consumer and even some foreign factory workers. But there are still some groups who would benefit from fewer sweatshops, namely American labor unions.

Unions are some of the biggest anti-sweatshop activists around.[11] How would they gain from higher wages and fewer jobs in the developing world? Well, as production fled from poor countries back to America, union workers would likely be the ones taking the higher paying jobs, driving up the cost of production.[12] So not only would developing economies lose jobs, but we as consumers would be paying more for our stuff.

We already see this phenomenon with things we buy every day in the United States. Often it looks innocent enough. The labels on things like T-shirts and coffee read "Union Made," "Sweat Free," or "Fair Trade." Translation: you're probably paying more for this item than you would be if it weren't produced under such restrictions.[13] Buying union-made products is effectively making a donation to the "American union member salary fund." There is nothing wrong with buying stuff like that—a consumer may prefer to pay extra to support a specific firm or type of producer. The problem arises when these products are marketed under false pretenses.

But simply asking people to buy union-made items is not enough for American unions. While there are those who are willing to pay more for American-made items, more price-sensitive consumers will tend to gravitate toward the cheaper product. As more union-made products are

---

10 Osorio, Ivan G. "How the Anti-Sweatshop Movement Hurts the People It Claims to Help." *IPA Review*, vol. 53, no. 4 (December 2001), p. 16.

11 The Union of Needletrades, Industrial and Textile Employees (UNITE)'s anti-sweatshop initiative is called Behind the Label (www.behindthelabel.org), and the American Federation of Labor and Congress of Industrial Organizations (AFL-CIO) has a "corporate watch" against sweatshops right on its Web site (www.aflcio.org/corporatewatch/stop/).

12 Input substitution again—this time with skilled (American) union labor substituting for less-skilled (foreign) labor.

13 Sometimes these labels can be (but aren't always) subject to certain higher quality standards as well (e.g., organic, grown without pesticides, not chemically altered), which probably accounts for some of the recent spike in the popularity of these type of products. Overpriced or not, the "Fair Trade" label and others like it may actually be a good indicator of quality. The dynamics of these new markets are still evolving, but they prompt some interesting economic questions, especially given their success thus far.

sold at higher prices, fewer factories and jobs can be sustained in the developing world. But a union slogan like "AFL-CIO: Keeping Poor Factory Workers Poor" just wouldn't have popular appeal.

So how can unions completely eliminate their overseas competition and get our business back? They *could* cut costs by working for less. Except they won't. Not too many union members want to pay dues only to have their leaders negotiate wages equal to what they could get without unionizing (i.e., in the competitive labor market). So unions generally hold out for wages that are not only higher than those in the developing world but higher than those in comparable, nonunionized jobs.

Demanding higher wages would be fine as long as union members were matching wage increases with productivity increases.[14] And while it's true that U.S. factory workers are often more productive per hour than workers in developing countries, the fact that factories and jobs are leaving the United States for the developing world is a good indication that some unions are not being efficient *enough* or pricing their workers' services attractively enough to compete.

Since they can't (or won't) match the cost-effectiveness of factories in the developing world, unions put a different spin on the issue to win over American consumers. They tell us that sweatshops are immoral. Ignoring the opportunities that sweatshops offer in poor countries, unions try to convince us that paying a textile worker in Bangladesh $0.13 an hour is inherently wrong—even if that same worker could only get $0.12 an hour (or less) working elsewhere.

And if enough American consumers can be convinced that foreign sweatshops are immoral, our demand for their products will decline. I saw this firsthand while working on a fundraiser for a service trip to Mexico. The idea was to sell T-shirts and donate the proceeds to a humanitarian organization in Mexico as a part of our service work.

When ordering the T-shirts, we had a choice: Pay $7 apiece for shirts that were actually made in Mexico or $11 each for shirts that were "union made" in the United States. The group leader chose to order the pricier shirts, saying, "It's worth a little extra money to know that these shirts were made under fair working conditions."

I think this is a sentiment shared by many Americans. My group leader's thought process was this: "I'm spending an extra $4 per shirt to make sure that Mexican factory workers don't have to work in terrible conditions." What she didn't realize was that her decision to buy union-made shirts was, in a small way, reducing labor demand and wages in Mexico. The extra $4 per shirt was a donation to American union members, and the cost to Mexican factory workers might have been far greater.

In a sad irony, my group leader's attempt to help the needy in Mexico was more of a disservice than a service. Her gut feeling about Mexican sweatshops was that they are bad for native workers, when in actuality

---

14 Like the (nonunion) workers in Henry Ford's factory, mentioned earlier in footnote 3.

the opposite is true. As we've seen, workers who can't work in factories are often forced backward to their second-best option. Reducing the amount of T-shirts bought from Mexico (even just a little bit), reduces the amount of workers needed to make them. Our service trip was meant to spark private enterprise and create jobs in Mexico, not get rid of them.

This is the union strategy at its worst. Union-sponsored anti-sweatshop campaigns are not intended to help impoverished sweatshop workers; they're intended to eliminate them as competition. They can achieve this by either (a) promoting higher wages in foreign factories or (b) convincing Americans not to buy from foreign factories at all. Unfortunately, the misconceptions about such factories are so far-reaching that even those who truly want to help sweatshop workers—like my group leader—wind up hurting them instead.

Lower relative wages are an advantage for the developing world. They give companies the means to produce goods more cheaply, and they give workers the chance to earn a better living. If I were put in the position of a sweatshop worker, I think I'd make the same choices that many are making every day: I'd get up in the morning to work at a factory that pays me more than I can get elsewhere.

Those who advocate closing sweatshops, or paying so-called fair wages, are proposing that we take away that option. They're messing with the natural development of foreign economies by knocking them off the first step of the staircase and eliminating relatively good jobs. In the process they are making stuff more expensive for everyone, for the benefit of a few American unions. If we really want to help foreign countries develop, let's take advantage of the low wages that sweatshop workers will accept. They'll thank us, and we'll be better off in the process.

READ ON/JOIN UP

➢ The Brookings Institute wondered how investment in foreign countries affects workers in the developing world. For a detailed look at their research findings and conclusions, see:

Moran, Theodore H. *Beyond Sweatshops*. Washington, DC: Brookings Institution Press, 2002.

➢ For a compelling description of the many ways that globalization and offshoring help improve people's lives, read:

Friedman, Thomas L. *The World Is Flat*. New York: Picador, 2005.

➢ If you're interested in the fair trade movement, its roots, its economic impact, and where it may be headed, this book is great background. The writers are all involved in the fair trade movement in the UK, and their observations provide some insight into why fair trade might be effective (or ineffective) elsewhere, too:

Bowes, John (ed.), et al. *The Fair Trade Revolution*. New York: Pluto Press, 2011.

> For a quick link to the Web site discussing the topic below, please visit www.pearsonhighered.com/walters:
>> Paul Krugman, who won the Nobel Prize in Economics in 2008, describes the beneficial impact cheap labor has on the developing world in this quick and engaging article: "In Praise of Cheap Labor: Bad Jobs at Bad Wages Are Better than No Jobs at All."

QUESTIONS FOR DISCUSSION

1. Imagine you find an article on the Internet that says one of your favorite clothing companies is opening a new garment factory. The factory is located on the outskirts of a major city in a relatively poor, developing country. Describe how the opening of this factory might affect (economically and/or socially) each of these individuals: (a) a farmer who owns a small plot of land a couple of miles from the factory; (b) an affluent doctor who runs a practice in the major city; (c) an American union member who works for the apparel company; and (d) you (a consumer who buys clothes at the company's store in the mall).

2. Figure 10-1 in this chapter, which is based on the research of economic historian Angus Maddison, shows a pretty dramatic improvement in living standards in the world starting about 1820. Think about possible reasons why there was so little progress in this regard for so long prior to this date. In your view, what was holding us back? What changed in the early 1800s that contributed to so much rapid economic growth—first in the West and then elsewhere? What have been the consequences of this growth for lifespans and the quality of life?

3. The World Bank estimates that about 1.4 billion people, a quarter of the world's population, live on less than $1.25 per day (even when adjusted for "purchasing power parity" of different currencies); most live and work in the developing world. Why don't many workers in developing countries earn wages that are even close to those in developed countries? Can you think of any scenarios where trying to eliminate this "wage gap" might actually hurt residents of poor countries? Can you think of policies that might close this gap without causing harmful unintended consequences?

4. The chapter suggests that labor unions are, at least sometimes, acting in *their* self-interest when they advocate regulations or policies that require higher wages or better working conditions in developing countries, rather than in the interests of workers in those countries. Review this argument, and evaluate its logic critically. Are there

conditions under which higher wages in developing countries would *not* reduce employment opportunities there? If so, do you think such conditions apply today?

5. Next time you're in the grocery store, look around for items that carry the "Fair Trade" label. Fruit, chocolate, coffee, and tea are usually good places to start. Compare the fair trade items with similar items that are "conventional." (a) What countries do the items come from? (b) How do their prices and quality compare? (c) How are the products marketed (e.g., does the packaging talk about producer countries or the treatment of workers)? (d) Would you consider buying fair trade products? Why or why not? (e) Do you see any similarities between the fair trade agriculture movement and calls for fair wages and working conditions in sweatshops?

CHAPTER 11

Why Men Love Tools

Poverty at the Personal and National Levels

by John J. Walters

Give a man a fish and he eats for a day. Teach a man to fish and he eats for a lifetime.

—FORTUNE COOKIE CLICHÉ

Chapter Highlights

- Poverty Threshold / Poverty Rate
- Investment
- Physical Capital
- Human Capital
- Economic Freedom and Growth

My first job was at a tire shop, where I was a "general technician." While that's not exactly the best fit for a short, skinny 16-year-old, it taught me two valuable lessons: (1) There's real satisfaction to be had from identifying and solving a problem, and (2) earning a living can be really hard if you don't go to college. First jobs provide kids with three very valuable things: money, something to keep them out of trouble, and "experience."

Now that I'm about to earn my economics degree, I see how perfect that experience was. Believe me, it didn't feel so terrific when I was walking home exhausted and covered in grime and motor oil every day. But it did give me the motivation to really apply myself to my studies so that I wouldn't spend the rest of my life working my body to the limit while someone else made all the decisions (and kept most of the money). Trust me: Blue-collar workers *earn* their wages—don't let anybody tell you differently.

My job also provided me with a great metaphor for the concept of poverty. When I say this, please don't assume that I am suggesting that I grew up in poverty, or that just because I wasn't "raking in the dough" that I was in poverty. I was still living with my parents, watching their TVs, eating their food, driving their cars, benefiting from the family health insurance plan, and so on. I got to spend nearly every penny I earned on myself. Hardly what you would call poverty-stricken.

IT'S ALL RELATIVE ... EXCEPT WHEN IT'S ABSOLUTE

Before I get into what I learned about poverty while changing tires and performing basic automotive inspections, let's get some definitions down. First of all, "poverty thresholds" are estimates of the annual amount of cash income required at minimal standards to support (i.e., feed, clothe, and house) families of various sizes. The "official poverty rate" is the percentage of the population with incomes below these thresholds. As of 2009, the U.S. poverty threshold for a single parent with one child was $14,787 annually, and 14.3 percent of Americans were officially poor. Back in 2000, that rate was 11.3 percent.[1]

By contrast, the international poverty threshold is set far lower, at about US$456 a year (a daily wage of just $1.25!), as of 2008. The international poverty rate is much higher than that of the United States: Roughly 25 percent of those in the developing world live on less than US$1.25 per day.[2]

I've been lucky enough to do a good bit of traveling during my 21 years, and some of my most enduring memories involve scenes of poverty. One of the most jarring was in New Orleans (I was there a couple of years after Hurricane Katrina struck the area), but I've seen people suffering just as badly in my own backyard of Baltimore. We'd be fooling ourselves, however, to think that the kind of poverty we see in America is anything like that experienced elsewhere in the world.

A rather surprising study by the Heritage Foundation found that a large percentage of those below the official poverty line in this country have cable TV, heat their food in microwave ovens, drive their own cars, and, in some cases, own their own homes.[3] This is *not* meant to suggest that American poverty is not a problem. If you live in a poor household, you're very likely to be badly housed, suffer from a poor diet, have inadequate access to medical care, attend a low-quality school, and see college as unattainable as well as unaffordable.

But, with very few exceptions, no matter what class you fall into in America, you might count yourself as fortunate. We're well off compared

---

1 The official poverty rate is an "absolute" measure. Sometimes people talk about "relative" poverty by measuring the fraction of the population with incomes below, say, half of the average income in an area. But that can be misleading: If it's a very affluent area, that "relative threshold" might be enough for a very comfortable life, and if it's not, even an average household might not have enough cash to live on. For a good, short explanation of some of the issues in measuring poverty, see the University of Michigan's National Poverty Center Web site, "Poverty in the United States—Frequently Asked Questions," at www.npc.umich.edu/poverty/.

2 World Bank. "Data on Poverty and Inequality." Available at http://web.worldbank.org/WBSITE/EXTERNAL/TOPICS/EXTPOVERTY/EXTISPMA/0,,contentMDK:20205999~isCURL:Y~menuPK:435951~pagePK:148956~piPK:216618~theSitePK:384329,00.html.

3 For the full breakdown of some surprising percentages, see Johnson, Kirk, and Rector, Robert. "Understanding Poverty in America." Heritage Foundation, 2004. Available at: www.heritage.org/Research/Welfare/bg1713.cfm.

to the vast majority of the world's population. Right now, the World Bank estimates that 1.4 billion people in the developing world live below the aforementioned international poverty line of US$1.25 a day.[4] Think about what you would buy (or not buy) every day if all you had was a buck twenty-five, without any safety net at all—no wealthy friends, family, or banks to loan you anything. Then think about what might be done to improve your condition.

Pain Meds for a Broken Bone

Trying to fix the poverty problem has been a major preoccupation of economists for as long as there have *been* economists. Adam Smith wrote his famous *Wealth of Nations* the same year America declared independence. Almost two and a half centuries later, there's still a lot of poverty—which means this is very stubborn stuff. The idea that you can fix a developing country's lagging economy with a prescription based on a simple mathematical model doesn't seem to hold much water. Such tools might give you a rough idea of the direction policy should take, but each case is different—not just on a country level but on an individual one, too.

One cliché I've heard a lot during discussions about poverty is that "the problem with poor people is that they just don't have enough money." That might literally be true, but it certainly isn't the whole story. Not having enough to make ends meet is no doubt painful, so to dull the pain we provide welfare checks, food stamps, and other types of governmental or charitable aid.

But my argument here is that we shouldn't look at poverty as some exotic, incurable disease. It's more like a broken bone. Painful? Certainly. Incurable? Certainly not. We know that doctors have no trouble resetting broken bones, so we'd never think to just give a patient a morphine drip and tell him to cowboy up while his arm hangs in three pieces. We have very specific ways to treat fractures and breaks so the bones will heal. What I learned while working as an automotive technician is that we have very specific ways to "heal" poverty as well.

One thing that divides the political left and right is disagreement about whether a person's poverty is an "accident," the result of some systemic failure (callous capitalism or misguided government policy—take your pick), or a byproduct of poor individual choices. The truth, in any individual case, is that it can be any or all of the above.

---

4 World Bank. "2008 World Development Indicators: Poverty Data." Available at: http:// siteresources.worldbank.org/DATASTATISTICS/Resources/WDI08supplement1216.pdf. That US$1.25-per-day figure, by the way, is computed using the "purchasing power parity" (PPP) method, in which the cost of buying a particular bundle of goods is calculated for each country's currency, and that information is used to express the cost of living in each country in a common currency unit—in this case, the United States dollar.

Sometimes people become poor, literally, by accident: an incapacitating injury or illness, loss of a job. Sometimes "The Man" (read: government) stands in our way to prosperity—a subject I'll have more to say about later. But most Americans' lifetime earnings are greatly affected by both the choices they make on a day-to-day basis and the circumstances (or institutions) that surround them. We can take steps to make ourselves richer in the long run by building up a good resume or avoiding credit card debt (among other things), but we must not assume that *everyone* is given opportunities to improve themselves both personally and economically. An escape from poverty requires two things: investment and opportunity. The rest of this chapter is devoted to showing how people (individually and collectively) can make these investments and how countries can (and must) make them possible.

PERSONAL INVESTING 101

When I first started working at the car shop, I was assured that I wouldn't need to buy my own tools because the shop had a set that I could use. While this may have been true, I soon found that doing things with my bare hands was almost as productive as taking the time to track down the old and busted shop tools. When no one really owns something, it tends to get mistreated, lost, broken, or stolen—and that's exactly what happened on a regular basis there.

Because finding and working with the shop's tools was almost impossible, I invested in my own. One week into my job, and I had already become the proud owner of a basic set of mechanics tools, purchased from Home Depot for the equivalent of one afternoon's labor.[5] Immediately, I was able to pick up my pace and start earning more commissions.

The great thing about tools is that nearly anyone can be more productive if you hand him the right one and show him how to use it, at least to a point.[6] But knowledge is also a tool. So, to further increase my productivity, I started hanging around the mechanics when they did some simple jobs, like oil changes and battery replacements. It wasn't much, but it was a start.

Suddenly my status had jumped from "total newbie" to "barely skilled laborer." I had leveled up. Actually, what I had done was increase my know-how, which is a tool that can be quite expensive but one you get to carry around with you all the time.[7]

---

5 Economists would say that I invested in some *physical capital* here.

6 Even with my increased productivity and my new tools, I was still, when it came to cars, inexperienced. I could change tires, but I couldn't do anything else. A $5,000 Snap-On tool chest wouldn't have equipped me to rebuild a transmission, even if I technically had access to all the right tools.

7 And which economists refer to as *human capital*.

I could go on, but I think you can see where I'm going with this illustration of poverty. When I first started work, let's pretend that I was absolutely destitute. I had no money, no tools (physical capital), and no know-how (human capital). Luckily, I got a job as a technician and could use some loaner tools while I learned the ropes. Suddenly I was productive enough to earn some money.

Then, as I started investing in my own tools and built up some more know-how, I became productive enough to earn a little more. My standard of living increased while my expenditure of energy actually decreased. I didn't have to spend what had felt like hours each day searching for busted tools and asking very basic questions. Later, I left the job to pursue a college degree and even further increase my know-how.[8] My little tool collection has helped me through many minor repairs since then.

If we want to bring some real-deal economics into the mix here, we can represent my experience with a simple production function. My output (Q) was based on two factors: the tools at my disposal, or capital (K), and the work I put in, or labor (L). To put it mathematically: $Q = f(K,L)$ or "Output is a function of capital and labor." In this equation, K and L are *partners*. As K grew (every time I purchased new tools or learned how to do a new job, I was increasing my K), then L's effectiveness increased. And as my labor became more effective, my wages rose.

This isn't just the way individuals avoid poverty—it's how economies grow. We could say that I was "poor" in the beginning because I didn't have a job. But the reason I didn't have a job was because I didn't have any tools or know-how—or the chance to use them even if I had. Fortunately, I had an able body and a willingness to learn, which is often enough to give you a chance in this country.

But notice: There were also some things about my circumstances, and this country, that enhanced my chances of success. As able and willing as I was to invest and learn, that might not have mattered if, for example, I hadn't been paid partly on commission, which gave me an incentive to buy those tools. Or if my extra income had been heavily taxed or the tools taken away ("expropriated") for some reason, I might have made different choices. In other words, my poverty was solved by both my interest in improving productivity *and* by a well-built rewards system.

If you think about it, these life-changing opportunities are what those fortune cookies I quoted at the beginning of this chapter are always talking about. Being in poverty is not caused by not having fish but by being *unable to fish*, either because you don't know how or because someone else is stopping you. In other words, it's not a lack of goods (or cash) but a lack of physical and human capital and the opportunity to acquire and use these to earn a living.

---

8 I should mention here that I did not have to pay my own way through college (thanks to the "parental subsidy plan"). If I had had to do that, I probably wouldn't have gone. This is an important side note because it illustrates how important access to financial assistance is to people seeking to invest in their future.

CHANGE COMES FROM WITHIN

I know I've been overusing the clichés in this chapter, but if I had titled this section with what it's really about you probably would have stopped reading right then and there, and I wouldn't have blamed you. But here it is, the hidden title of this section: What we can learn from the Economic Freedom Index (EFI). To borrow the words of the study's sponsor, the Heritage Foundation, the EFI gauges "the fundamental rights of every human to control his or her own labor and property." In my own words: It measures a person's opportunity to earn a living.

If you really want to get technical, the EFI takes account of how much personal choice people around the world have in their own lives, their freedom to exchange goods and services, the legal protection of their property, the even-handed enforcement of contracts, the stability of the monetary environment (e.g., inflation), how much they pay in taxes, the existence of barriers to international trade (e.g., import taxes), and whether resources are allocated by the market (you, me, and our neighbors) or the government.

All right, that's a few too many economic ideas to take in all at once. But if you go through the list item by item, it's filled with stuff that we all want, even if we wouldn't normally sit around measuring it or even thinking about it. It's much easier to focus on political rights, like our right to free speech or to bear arms. Still, the right to choose how we spend our wages—and our right to earn wages at all—is of the utmost importance.

Once you've measured economic freedom, you can see how its presence—or absence—affects the quality of peoples' lives. And the key finding on that score is this: Countries with the highest economic freedom ratings generally have the highest standards of living and income growth rates.

In 2011, the United States' EFI placed ninth (actually down a notch from 2010, but still near the top of the "mostly free" list). The top five are Hong Kong, Singapore, Australia, New Zealand, and Switzerland. Our country may not be perfect, but it's still pretty good in terms of our freedom to work and trade. Not coincidentally, the countries with the lowest measures of economic freedom also have the lowest living standards and growth rates. The five least economically free countries in the world are Venezuela, Eritrea, Cuba, Zimbabwe, and North Korea; even the wealthiest of these (Venezuela) has a per capita income of only one-fourth that in the United States, and the rest are far poorer than that.[9]

China, which has experienced extremely fast-paced economic growth in recent years, has been making efforts to set aside large portions of their government-controlled economy to, in effect, become more like the very

---

9 Heritage Foundation. "2011 Index of Economic Freedom." Available at www.heritage.org/index/Ranking.

free (and prosperous) Hong Kong economy. These efforts have raised China's EFI score considerably, compared to where it was before the reforms began in 1980, but the country still scores below average on economic freedom, ranking 135th of 179 countries in 2011, and China's per capita income is still less than one-seventh that in the United States.[10]

The correlation between economic freedom and a thriving marketplace should come as no surprise. Economic freedom means, above all else, enhanced opportunity. It means that people will be able to start businesses like the tire shop where I worked, provide jobs for people (like me and a lot of other folks), accumulate capital (physical and human) to help them become more productive and prosperous, and use that capital in ways they see as most profitable or desirable.

Economies improve only when people are both able to grow and *benefit from their growth*. Less economic freedom means fewer businesses, and fewer businesses means reduced job opportunities. A man with a full tool chest but no job will remain in poverty.[11] Physical and human capital are both important, but they can be useless in the wrong circumstance or without opportunity.

This is what I mean by "The Man" standing in the way of prosperity. Governments play the primary role in establishing healthy economies and preserving economic freedom for their citizens. They are the gatekeepers to the growth that poor people so desperately need.[12]

THE (ONLY) SIMPLE SOLUTION

So what's my solution? It certainly isn't any new equation or calculus-driven model that promises results if only a certain amount of foreign aid (read: pain medicine for the broken bone) is funneled into a struggling country. It'll take a lot more than money for countries like Haiti (ranked 133rd in EFI in 2011) and Iran (171st) to turn their disastrous economies around. Like China, the citizens of these countries need deep-seated economic reforms

---

10 If you are wondering why their rating isn't higher, given their growth, keep in mind that only about 30 percent of the population has found work in these Special Economic Zones (SEZ). The rest of the economy is still run by the government, which puts a damper on their ratings and their growth. In an SEZ, tax rates are kept at zero until a company begins to earn a profit. Then, after 2 years of profit, a company pays 50 percent of the normal tax rate for the next 2 years. After that, taxes are assessed as normal. For more information on how China is stifling its own growth, see the Heritage Foundation's explanation: www.heritage.org/index/Country/China.

11 This might explain why we seem to have had such rotten luck with foreign aid. We spend money to send expensive tool chests (metaphorically speaking) to people in poor countries when what we should be doing is working with local governments to provide these people with greater economic freedom so that they can apply those tools to productive uses.

12 For a great study on "The Man" keeping poor people down, read Hall, Joshua C., Sobel, Russell S., and Crowley, George R. "Institutions, Capital, and Growth." Available at www.be.wvu.edu/div/econ/work/pdf_files/10-15.pdf.

that allow them to begin to take hold of their own destinies, solve their own problems, and create their own fortunes.[13]

How? The same way I did. By taking advantage of an opportunity and then working to acquire physical and human capital—tools and know-how. What studies of economic freedom have taught us is that poverty goes hand in hand with a lack of these essential elements and conditions that encourage and reward their development. When citizens of an economically repressed country are kept from acquiring and using capital, either from a lack of opportunity or because they don't see the potential benefit to their own lives, their entire economies are kept from growing.

I'm not the only one advocating such an approach, either. In fact, it is by no means a new idea. Late economist Peter Bauer wrote several book on poverty and development in the post-WWII era, and much of his work challenged the prevailing viewpoint that poverty could be effectively combated by strong but misguided central governments or with massive infusions of foreign aid dollars.

LET'S NOT GET AHEAD OF OURSELVES

Rapid income growth isn't a cure-all.[14] It doesn't mean that people's lives will suddenly be improved to a level of which Americans—even poor Americans—would approve. Poor countries have a long, hard road to travel, but traveling it is better than standing still. And it's certainly better than throwing more "painkiller" cash at another country that just isn't set up to grow. We need to be focused on helping countries enact financial and political reforms that allow poor people around the world to increase their worth through productive endeavors. Fighting for these basic building blocks would be a much better use of our foreign aid dollars.

Part of the reason there are so many subsistence farmers in poor countries around the world is that there just aren't many other opportunities. It's unlikely that businesses are going to be set up to provide those opportunities when they know that they are going to be taxed to death or told how to run their business by crooked, bumbling bureaucrats.

For someone to get a job, a system must exist where people who have jobs to offer can freely transact with those who wish to sell their labor. The best examples of this are the Special Economic Zones in China that are now host to hundreds upon hundreds of factories with abundant job opportunities that churn out products for people all over the world. They have helped millions of people get off the farm. The reason America is

---

13 To say this in economic terms: save, invest, acquire physical and human capital, earn higher wages, and repeat.

14 It is difficult to tell how much progress is really made in a country just by looking at GDP growth, as this ignores things like a widening income gap or pollution output. Like I said before, any discussion about poverty is complicated.

thought of as the Land of Opportunity is because it is (or was) so economically free and its property rights so secure that our entire country could be considered one big Special Economic Zone. That means growth—and lots of it.

Establishing the institutions of economic freedom—where people will be properly rewarded for improving themselves, their property rights are secure, and they can trade freely and efficiently—is what poor countries need to do if they want to break the cycle of poverty. Imagine how much the nation of China is benefitting from all those folks who got off the farm and are now working more productively and earning more money. The phrase "economic growth" should be getting much more concrete and understandable now. It's really just a fancy term for all the human improvements that allow a country to become more affluent, more livable, and more comfortable.

From my own personal experience, I've seen how economic freedom and opportunity work to my benefit, as I hope you have in your own life. We all know this works on an individual level—it's what allows people to get jobs, sometimes change them until they are happy, and get good enough at them to make (almost!) enough money to buy what they want. When you give people the opportunity to be properly rewarded for acquiring the right tools and know-how, good things happen and people usually get richer. At that point, the broken bone can begin to heal.

Read On/Join Up

➤ This book is a recent bestselling examination of the complex interaction between individual choice and opportunity. Gladwell has a very easy-to-understand writing style that makes complex ideas simple, profound, and extremely interesting. See:

Gladwell, Malcolm. *Outliers: The Story of Success.* New York: Little, Brown & Company, 2008.

➤ For quick links to the Web sites discussed below, please visit www. pearson*highered.com/walters*:

Poverty Newsblog is a factual and current blog about the way poverty is experienced around the world.

Defeat Poverty contains the author's thoughts on how we could best combat poverty worldwide in blog format and with links to a few of the author's published works. Although I have not read his books, his work seems compelling and worth checking into if the subject is of interest to you.

Questions for Discussion

1. What tools and know-how are you acquiring right now? Think about your education, your work experience, and what you do in your

spare time. How are you investing in your own human capital or acquiring physical capital? How would your answer be different if you had chosen not to attend college, or perhaps even if you had decided simply to attend a different school?

2. The official poverty rate is an attempt to measure "absolute poverty," while statistics on the distribution of income (such as the fraction of total national income received by particular segments of the population) get at "relative poverty." Which concept do you think is more important? Suppose, for example, that a country's official poverty rate was 12 percent, while the poorest one-fifth of its population received only 5 percent of total national income and the richest one-fifth received 40 percent of national income. If a proposed policy change could (somehow) double the *share* of total income going to the poorest fifth of the population (to 10 percent) but also increased the official poverty rate to, say, 15 percent, would you consider this a worthwhile tradeoff?

3. If someone told you that you had one year to help get one individual out of poverty with only the resources you have right now, what would you do? Would you try to help someone locally or reach out to someone internationally? Would your involvement be personal or mainly financial? How could you adapt that solution to help people on a larger scale?

4. Economists use equations called "production functions" to describe how inputs such as physical capital (K) and labor (L) combine to produce output (Q). Suppose, for example, that Dormitoria's production function is $Q = 10KL$. If there are 10 units of K and 50 units of L, what will Dormitoria's total output (Q) be? If foreign aid allows Dormitoria to double its K stock to 20, how much would you predict Q to rise? In the real world (i.e., the one that is more complex than can be described by such a simple equation), what kinds of complications might arise that would prevent this happy result from occurring?

5. Do some online research to see which countries' levels of economic freedom (as measured by the EFI) have been rising or falling most significantly in recent years. How have such changes correlated with these countries' standards of living over the same period?

CHAPTER 12

Land of the Free

Regulation, Redistribution, and Rights

by Crystal A. Callahan

Most people want security in this world, not liberty.

—H. L. MENCKEN,
MINORITY REPORT, 1956

Chapter Highlights

- Tradeoffs
- Optimization vs. Maximization
- Equity vs. Efficiency
- Income Redistribution
- Insurance

If you've ever been to a baseball game, you know the routine. On the way to our seats, we buy an obligatory hot dog, some popcorn, an overpriced draft beer or soda, and maybe a foam finger to wave around. Then, just after we sit down, the PA announcer tells us to stand back up for the national anthem.

And if you're like me, at first you're thinking more about that juicy hot dog than the lyrics, and you wish that the singer would hurry it up already. But the anthem can be quite moving if sung by the right person. Especially toward the finale—"O'er the land of the free!" is the big line, and it can be enough to provoke a patriotic tear in even the manliest of men. Of course, it's not just the impressive high note that moves game spectators and players—maybe it has to do with the fondness we feel toward our freedom.

Or, at least, the fondness I *thought* we had for our freedom.

I had an interesting conversation with a friend of mine a while back. She was adamantly opposed to drug legalization, and I was trying to explain some of the consequences of prohibition.

"When the government prohibits things, doesn't that take away some of our freedom to make personal choices?" I asked her.

"Obviously," she responded, "but we shouldn't be allowed to make bad choices anyway."

"Why not? Isn't America supposed to be the land of the free? Shouldn't we be allowed to make whatever choice we want?" I countered.

"No, America isn't the land of the free," she said simply. "It's the government's responsibility to limit our choices to make sure we don't hurt ourselves."

I admit I was surprised by how quickly my friend was willing to leave her freedom in the hands of the government. It got me thinking: Isn't our freedom a basic concept rooted in our understanding of what it is to be American, or is it more complicated? To find some answers, this chapter examines freedom from an economic perspective, including a discussion of tradeoffs, optimization vs. maximization, equity vs. efficiency, Pareto optimality, and incentives and work effort.

Bargain Hunters

Something occurred to me after speaking with my friend: Maybe some of us see our freedom as a bargaining chip. Maybe what my friend meant was that she'd be happy to give up *some* of her individual freedom in exchange for something she liked even better. She treated freedom just like any other good, and she was arguing that there is an *optimal* amount of freedom that is good for society and that it's not the same as the *maximum* amount. If we maximized our consumption of any one good, we'd sacrifice an awful lot of other things, probably spending far more on that good than it is really worth. Nice clothes make me happy, but I don't spend *all* my money accumulating the best possible wardrobe; I need to eat, too. I optimize rather than maximize my happiness from clothes and save some of my budget for other things that might deliver more value than a closet that rivals Carrie Bradshaw's.

Similarly, freedom is not an all-or-nothing good. My friend was displaying her willingness to trade a bit of freedom for something she thought she might value more: a safer, "drug-free" America. In her view, if the government allowed us to experience freedom to the max, drug regulations would have to go. Call it the "safety-freedom tradeoff." We lose a right, but (hopefully!) gain some protection from harm.

A related concept is what economists call the "equity-efficiency tradeoff." Sometimes, for example, we're willing to make the country run a little less efficiently by taxing some activities to improve the living standards of the needy (e.g., by supplying food stamps, medical care, or housing subsidies). We lose some output in the taxed market in exchange for less poverty or, more generally, greater fairness or equity.[1]

---

1 Taxes usually have three effects: a higher (after-tax) price to buyers, lower (after-tax) receipts for sellers, and a reduction in the amount exchanged, which results in additional losses to both buyers and sellers that economists call "deadweight welfare loss." In sum, buyers and sellers in the taxed market give up more of their potential gains from exchange than will ultimately be transferred to the beneficiaries of any public program, thanks to this deadweight loss.

What's the problem here? Shouldn't we rationally give up a right here or there if it'll make the world a safer or fairer place overall? We do something similar every time we go through security at the airport. In our quest to make flying safer for everyone, we give up some time, pack our toiletries in little baggies, and occasionally submit to the (super) embarrassing full-body scan. We may not *like* it—I'd certainly prefer to get extra safety without giving up anything to get it—but in the real world, most of us are willing to make that compromise.

We also make this tradeoff every time we go to the beach. Imagine how upset you'd be if some bratty kid falsely yelled "SHARK!" while you were enjoying the water. Picturing a giant great white straight out of *Jaws*, everyone would rush to get on the sand as fast as they could. Some might be trampled, some would scratch and claw their way to safety, and some might be left behind to face the fictitious shark, and all for nothing. Maybe that kid would be entertained by watching the mass hysteria, but most people would be pretty angry.

Some people would probably want the kid to be punished for his stunt. But wasn't he just exercising his freedom of speech rights? Technically, yes—but perhaps he was exercising it a little too much. Maximum freedom of speech on the beach leads to an undesirable and potentially chaotic outcome. In short, beachgoers are willing to sacrifice their freedom to yell out whatever they want on the beach to ensure a safe and peaceful day in the sun. There's an optimal level of freedom of speech on the beach that imposes some limits on the prankster so that everyone else can relax.

The U.S. Supreme Court supports economists on the "optimize rather than maximize" issue. In *Schenck v. United States*,[2] Justice Oliver Wendell Holmes opined for a unanimous Court that when words used in particular circumstances tend to create a "clear and present danger" of a riot, such words are not protected by the First Amendment of the Constitution. As an example, Justice Holmes described an instance of an individual falsely yelling "FIRE!" in a crowded theater. Such speech is not protected because it simply serves to foster false panic. Justice Holmes recognized the distinction between maximum enforcement of First Amendment rights and optimum enforcement. If we optimize, the value of the small amount of freedom we give up is exceeded by the value of what we get in return, which is a safer, more relaxing theater experience. While the Supreme Court later limited the *Schenck* holding (in *Brandenburg v. Ohio*[3]) to apply to cases in which banned speech is likely to lead to "imminent danger" (such as a riot), the optimization rationale remains the same.

---

2 249 U.S. 47 (1919).
3 395 U.S. 444 (1969).

The Big (X-ray) Picture

While it may *seem* easy to figure out the optimal policy regarding free speech rights at a crowded movie theater or beach, most tradeoffs between things we value highly—freedom and safety or prosperity and fairness—are controversial and difficult to evaluate. Ideally, we'd like the exchange to make *everyone* better off. That is, if we put such a compromise to a vote, it'd win unanimously. But that might be too much to ask for in the real world. Even in my beach example, maybe the prankster would complain that he values his right to prank more than we all value our extra safety from limiting his speech.

Think back to the example regarding airport security. The new X-ray scanners have gotten a lot of bad press, as many believe full-body scans violate their right to privacy. In fact, a slew of products have emerged so that people can cover up what they don't want seen by Transportation Security Administration agents. Undergarments with messages such as "For my eyes only" are advertised on quite a few of my favorite blog and shopping Web sites. Those who are outraged by the scanners consider the costs of this invasion of their privacy to be greater than the additional security benefits. For them, being required to pass through a typical metal detector might be okay, but this new technology provides too much safety and too little privacy.

On the other hand, those who don't mind the scan likely believe the incremental safety increase is well worth the decrease in freedom.[4] As a result, it'll be very difficult to figure out the right balance to strike—the "optimum"—in cases like this. Not only might there be no arrangement of rights that will meet with unanimous approval, but occasionally there might be none that even wins a popular consensus.

What to do? Well, one approach might be to go back to the drawing board and try to find some new arrangement of rights when the one you've proposed isn't gaining widespread approval. In fact, that's often what policymakers do: If one tradeoff is unpopular, invent another. The overall goal should be to achieve a desired improvement in safety with the least amount of freedom lost. Of course, as in the case of TSA scanners, policymakers sometimes also take the approach of telling opponents of a policy that they're essentially out of luck if they do not like

---

4 In other words, they believe the marginal benefit of submitting to the scan exceeds its marginal cost. Economists believe people make decisions (or ought to) by comparing the increase in satisfaction (or, in econ-speak, the "marginal utility") received from additional consumption to its incremental (marginal) cost. The "law of diminishing marginal utility" suggests that as we consume more of anything (within a given period of time), our total satisfaction may rise, but it's by smaller and smaller amounts. Therefore, even if the marginal cost of additional consumption is not rising, we'll eventually say, "Enough!" For instance, we might decide that we don't value an additional unit of safety as much as it costs in inconvenience or reduced privacy.

it. Currently, if you don't want to be scanned then you likely can't fly, either.[5]

HOMERUN!

Equity-efficiency tradeoffs can be even trickier than freedom-for-safety swaps.

Let's return to that ballpark we visited earlier. It's a big game, and with incredible timing, I begin to make my way to the concession stand for another draft beer (don't worry, I'm legal) when a homerun ball comes flying my way! Instead of following my instinct to dodge, I gather myself, put my old fielder's mitt out to shield my face, and ... miraculously catch it! My heroics are even broadcast on the Jumbotron for the crowd to see, and they cheer.

Better still, a sports memorabilia collector dashes up, saying something about a "historic milestone," and offers me $1,000 for the ball. I quickly close the deal and ecstatically wave the money at my friends.

To my surprise, they don't seem happy for me but . . . jealous. A couple of them mumble congrats, but then one of my more outspoken friends blurts out, "Ya know, Crystal, it's not fair you got that money. I mean, I was just letting you get by me so you could go get more beer, and you lucked out! I would've caught it if you hadn't been in my way."

"Hah! Luck had nothing to do with it!" I gloat, waving my mitt. "I came prepared." Eyeing the "Phillies #1!" foam hand with the pointing index finger that she was wearing, I add, "Besides, no way you catch anything with a foam hand. I probably saved you from getting a couple of broken fingers." At that there's a low murmur of disapproval from the rest of my friends. Okay, I took it too far. But what's wrong with everybody all of a sudden? Instead of celebrating my terrific catch and new wealth, we all sit gloomily and silently.

Eventually, I figure out the problem. I'm focused on the preparation and skill I showed in catching the ball. I overcame my fear and risked injury and embarrassment to *earn* that $1,000. But my friends are equally focused on how lucky I was to be in the right place at the right time.

And I have to admit that they have a point. I *was* in front of my friend when the ball happened to arrive; if I hadn't been there, maybe she would have caught it, or maybe one of the guys on her right or left would have instead. What's more, none of us bothered to match our seat numbers to our tickets before we sat down, so her seat might technically belong to

---

5 Another approach that economists take is to try to determine a "Pareto efficient" or "Pareto optimal" result. A Pareto efficient allocation of goods or resources among individuals is one in which no *redistribution* can make one person better off without making another person worse off. If we're dealing with safety and freedom, we have achieved Pareto efficiency only if, for example, the extra bit of safety I might prefer won't make someone else upset.

one of the other members of our group. Hmm. Maybe taking my "earn-ings" and splitting them up among all of us *is* the right thing to do.

But wait. Just as I'm feeling guilty about hogging the ball, I think about what might have happened if I'd known we were going to share the proceeds equally. I would have never taken the chance of getting hit (glove or not, that ball is a missile!). The smart play might have been just to duck, hope that one of my friends caught it, and wait for my fair share. But if I had ducked, there might be nothing to share at all. If all of my friends had ducked, too, the ball would have very likely ricocheted around, and someone a few rows away might have the thousand bucks instead of our group. Or, maybe one of the guys in our group would have stepped up to impress the girls around us regardless of the distribution arrangement. This is tougher than I thought.

It's also important. The tradeoff I'm grappling with now is at the heart of the debate regarding government programs to redistribute wealth in society. Those who favor taxing the rich heavily and redistributing those taxes to the poor, Robin Hood style, tend to think the rich are mostly lucky. Maybe they have good genes to get them into the movies or height to help out on the basketball court. Or, perhaps they were born to parents who could afford to send them to top schools, which led to lucrative job offers. Or, like me and my mitt, they happened to be standing in the right spot when money fell from the sky, like Wall Street traders during the technology boom.

On one hand, people like me tend to highlight how we prepared, took risks, worked hard, or otherwise earned our money, and we think we deserve to keep it. We don't see why anyone, from our friends to the government, is entitled to take away the fruits of our labor and pass it around. And we'd make two points in our defense: Redistributing our wealth doesn't seem fair to *us*, and it might be counterproductive. If I don't make the effort to get the ball, remember, there will probably be nothing to redistribute.

On the other hand, good fortune *does* play a role in how we make out in life. One of the richest people in the world, Microsoft founder Bill Gates, usually explains his success by saying "I was lucky."[6] Gates doesn't just mean he was born smart. He understands that he was born in the right place at the right time and went to a high school that had enough money to buy computers in the early days of the tech revolution. It was mainly due to those opportunities that he learned how to program when very few people in the industry could. If he'd gone to a different high school, or grown up before the computer industry needed programmers, or after accessible and efficient programming had already been developed, we might never have heard of Bill Gates. So luck and timing are important,

---

6 Gladwell, Malcolm. *Outliers: The Story of Success.*, New York: Little, Brown & Co., 2008, pp. 50–55.

but so are preparation, talent, and effort. Furthermore, if we lived in a world where we taxed all of Bill Gates's fortune away, he may have never bothered learning how to program at all, just as I may have never tried to catch the ball if I knew I had to share the $1,000.

The "Moral" of the Story

So where does this leave us? It looks like equity-efficiency tradeoffs are a high-wire act. Leaning too far in either direction is costly, and finding the right balance won't be easy.

Why suffer through the balancing act? Maybe you're thinking, "Why trade any efficiency for 'fairness' at all? Lucky or not, once I've made my money, it should stay mine. Anything else is *un*fair."

But consider this: What if my friends and I had thought about fairness before that homerun was hit, or even before we showed up for the game? We might have agreed beforehand to split the proceeds of a possible catch to increase everyone's chance of walking away with something. This is the guiding idea behind coworkers who enter into lottery pools together. That kind of voluntarily-agreed-upon deal is like buying insurance. Each of us stands a better chance of walking away with *some*thing, though maybe a smaller something than one of us might have taken away if we relied on our own efforts.

Outside a ballpark, in the real world, it's quite a bit harder to decide *beforehand* which side of the redistribution issue we might fall on. Most of us don't know early in life whether we'll end up rich or poor. Once we *know* we're a talented 7'2" basketball player, or a programming genius, or the heir to a successful business we might naturally prefer that all our income remains in our possession. But what if we have to vote on a redistribution policy before we know how our life story will end? If there's a chance we might grow up in an impoverished family with little opportunity to make anything of ourselves or squander what we manage to make early in our lives, perhaps a bit of help would be nice. Given that kind of uncertainty, some of us might choose to buy an insurance policy and vote for income redistribution as a way to reduce our risk of being desperately poor.

In deciding beforehand to "level the playing field," we might hurt our chances of using our individual talents to make ourselves and society richer. The monetary incentive to effectively utilize our individual talents, to take risks, and to work hard would be reduced. If we take redistribution too far, some important incentives might disappear. Economists have been studying the effects of tax policy on work effort for a long time, and there's plenty of evidence that shows that we do not work as hard when we get to keep less of our earnings. For example, Edward Prescott, who shared the 2004 Nobel Prize in Economics, has found that "Americans on a per person aged 15–64 basis work in the market sector 50 percent more than the French," that "low labor supplies in Germany, France, and Italy are due to high tax rates," and, as a result, "U.S. output per person is about 40 percent higher than in the European countries."[7]

So here we are, in a time and place in which regulatory and redistributive policies are the subject of intense debate and disagreement. Some people, such as my friend, advocate giving up freedom or wealth to the government because they believe the sacrifice will result in a safer or more fair society overall. She has made a rational decision to prefer additional safety over maximum freedom.[8] Drug laws certainly reduce our personal freedom, but maybe the country is a safer place due to these restrictions. We cannot yell whatever we want in a crowded theater, but do not have to worry about needless riots. We may not be able to zip through security at the airport, but fewer terrorists will make it onto our planes. Not as many of us might get rich, but fewer people will be poor.

However, giving up freedom or wealth doesn't *guarantee* greater security or equity; we have to be very careful about such tradeoffs. Economists can't provide a definitive recommendation about how much safety or freedom is optimal in every case. As we've seen throughout this book, there are compelling reasons to let individuals make free choices in markets and cogent arguments about why governmental limits on those choices can enhance our welfare.

What the tools of economic analysis *can* do is help us understand the rationales underlying both sides of this great debate and enable us to make better informed choices about particular policies. It won't always be easy, and we won't always agree, but if we want to make good decisions individually and socially, we simply don't have a choice. As philosopher Blaise Pascal said, "Let us endeavor, then, to think well: this is the mainspring of morality."

READ ON/JOIN UP

➤ For a philosophical perspective on liberty and equality, see:
  Rawls, John. *A Theory of Justice*. Cambridge, MA: Belknap of Harvard University Press, 1971.

  Rawls, John, and Kelly, Erin. *Justice as Fairness: A Restatement*. Cambridge, MA: Harvard University Press, 2001.

---

7 In a nutshell, Americans produce more goods and services because we work more, not because we're more productive in the hours we work. If you're thinking, "Well, the Europeans are just more laid back culturally than us," Prescott points out that as recently as the 1970s, Europeans actually worked *more* hours than Americans. Funny how culture can be affected by tax policy. See: Prescott, Edward C., "Why Do Americans Work So Much More than Europeans?" *Federal Reserve Bank of Minneapolis Quarterly Review*, vol. 28, no. 1 (July 2004), pp. 3, 7.

8 Another point to consider is the concept of bounded rationality. Based on the amount and quality of information available, time allotted to make decisions, and individuals' varying cognitive capabilities, some decisions may not be fully rational.

➢ For a libertarian answer to John Rawls, favoring a "minimalist state," see:
> Nozick, Robert. *Anarchy, State, and Utopia*. New York: Basic, 1974.

➢ For a look into collective preference and decision procedures, see:
> Sen, Amartya. *Collective Choice and Social Welfare*. San Francisco: Holden-Day, 1970.

➢ A discussion of how important freedom is to a functional, vibrant marketplace can be found here:
> Gersemann, Olaf. *Cowboy Capitalism: European Myths, American Reality*. Washington, DC: Cato Institute, 2004.

➢ For quick links to Web sites regarding the topics below, please visit *www.pearsonhighered.com/walters*:
> A real-world parallel involving the CAFE standards for automobile fuel usage and the resulting highway safety decline can be explored at Heritage Org and National Center Org.

> On the balance between personal privacy and airline safety, see ABC News Blog, UCSD Guardian Org, and TSA.

QUESTIONS FOR DISCUSSION

1. Where do you stand in the debate regarding use of full body scanners at airports by the Transportation Safety Administration (TSA)? The chapter argues that we should "achieve a desired improvement in safety with the least amount of freedom lost." Some might say, however, that in this case compromising safety even a little bit might lead to loss of life, so "optimization" and "maximization" policies would (or should) be the same: Take every step, no matter how intrusive, that delivers even a tiny improvement in safety. Do you agree? Why or why not?

2. Consider three public policies (A, B, and C) that will have effects on both a country's income (will affect "efficiency") and the amount of perceived fairness (or "equity") its citizens enjoy. Policy A will increase efficiency by 10 percent but reduce equity by 10 percent; Policy B will decrease efficiency by 10 percent but increase equity by 10 percent; Policy C will decrease both efficiency and equity by 10 percent. Rank these policies according to their desirability to you; explain your choices. Can you think of any general rules that policymakers should follow in evaluating alternatives like this? Is there any additional information you'd like about this country before you make up your mind about ranking these policies?

3. The chapter cites "lottery pools" as an example of voluntary risk pooling or buying insurance: When you join such a pool, you limit

your "upside" potential but increase the chances you'll win something rather than nothing. Now suppose a friend of yours, after reading about a successful lottery pool in the paper, comes up with an ingenious business plan: She is going to start a "life lottery pool." She will sell shares in this pool to 99 classmates ("Some of whom are destined to be rich hedge-fund managers, some starving artists—we don't know which right now," she says). Then, for the rest of their lives, they will all *pool* their incomes, after which she will distribute 1/100th of the total to each member (keeping one share for herself, as a reward for the awesomeness of her idea and payment for administering the pool). Constructively critique your friend's plan. (Note: *Assume it's legal and the contract that members sign will be binding.*) Analyze why and to whom it might be appealing and how it might work in practice.

4. Discuss whether and why you believe that policymakers (or the courts) have determined the "optimal" tradeoff (e.g., of freedom vs. safety, or regarding keeping our earnings vs. alleviating others' poverty) in these cases: (a) we can't yell "fire" in a crowded movie theater except under certain circumstances; (b) in many states, we can't talk on handheld cell phones while driving; (c) we pay higher marginal tax rates as our income rises; (d) in many states we can't ride a motorcycle without wearing a helmet.

5. In recent years, economists have been making a great deal of progress incorporating some insights of psychologists into economic models of choice. In some cases, this work has suggested that human beings actually have a tough time processing all the information required to make a good decision (which economists have identified as "bounded rationality"). And some researchers even suggest that we might occasionally prefer to be confronted with *fewer* rather than more choices when we make decisions. Identify some examples from your own life where you have had a tough time comparing alternative choices because of "information overload" and/or situations where you've thought, "I have too many choices." Is there anything you can think of that we can or should do about such problems?

INDEX